Sustaining Affirmation

Sustaining Affirmation

THE STRENGTHS OF WEAK ONTOLOGY IN POLITICAL THEORY

Stephen K. White

PRINCETON UNIVERSITY PRESS
PRINCETON AND OXFORD

Published by Princeton University Press, 41 William Street,
Princeton, New Jersey 08540
In the United Kingdom: Princeton University Press,
3 Market Place, Woodstock, Oxfordshire OX20 1SY

Library of Congress Cataloging-in-Publication Data

White, Stephen K.
Sustaining affirmation : the strengths of weak ontology in
political theory / Stephen K. White.
p. cm.
ISBN 0-691-05032-5 (alk. paper) — ISBN 0-691-05033-3 (pbk. : alk. paper)
1. Political science—Philosophy. 2. Ontology. I. Title.
JA71.W457 2000
320′.01—dc21 00-021160

This book has been composed in Baskerville

The paper used in this publication meets the minimum requirements of ANSI/NISO Z39.48-1992 (R1997) (*Permanence of Paper*)

www.pup.princeton.edu

Printed in the United States of America

1 3 5 7 9 10 8 6 4 2

To Cam

who goes carefully into the world

CONTENTS

PREFACE

IMAGINE YOURSELF standing by a vacant lot watching children play. Debris lies about, for a building once stood here, until its foundation gave way. Chunks of the building remain here and there, as does the gaping hole left from the foundation. As the children clamber over the remains and jump in and out of the hole, you begin to think that they are playing a game, but it is one with which you are unfamiliar. In fact, the rules still seem to be emerging, and the children themselves are sometimes uncertain how to proceed. It would be pretty difficult, accordingly, to give a decent account of this game.

Despite your doubts, you venture a speculation about the rules. But immediately your uncertainty increases again when another adult passes and, with an air of authority, informs you, "That's not really a game. Not enough coherence." A second passerby curtly announces that the children ought not, in any case, to be playing in such a dangerous lot. A third passerby eyes you with some impatience before offering the rebuke, "Must one always try to foist some underlying structure onto what should be simply free play?"

What to do? Aware of the risks, you decide to go ahead and reflect further about what still looks to you like a game, and a good one at that. A plausible start might be to focus on three or four kids who seem to be the most comfortable with the game, the closest to being competent in their negotiation of the still somewhat amorphous rules. Your hope is that in attending carefully to that competence, you can make the rules more palpable. If this can be done well, you will be satisfied for the moment.

That, anyway, is what I have tried to do in this book. The new game being played is not, of course, children in a vacant lot, but contemporary ways of entwining ontological reflection with political affirmation. Call the game "weak ontology." It is taking place on the terrain of what used to be called the "foundations" of ethics and politics, the sources from which affirmative gestures gain their strength.[1] Now obviously not every affirmation of a specific value or practice has to be traced back to such a source. A particular, discrete argument may be all that is necessary to defend our preference for, say, a given democratic practice. We are nevertheless sometimes pushed to articulate more extensively how we

[1] I specifically do not say that one's weak ontology is the privileged starting point for justification; more on this issue will be said in chapter 1.

justify that affirmation. At those moments, we think of ourselves as enriching the persuasiveness of our claims. Political theory has traditionally understood this activity as one of having recourse to foundations. My aim in this book is to help rethink this "having recourse to," both in terms of how one does it and the character of that to which recourse is had.

My strategy is to clarify the coherence of the new game of "weak ontology" a bit further with the help of some philosophical players who have ventured onto the vacant lot. The four players I examine occupy, in conventional terms, very different perspectives: liberal, communitarian, feminist, and poststructuralist or postmodern. Without denying the importance of the differences, I want to draw out certain commonalities that emerge when one asks how each thinker configures the background that sustains his or her affirmative political gestures. Methodologically, I am continually engaged in the hermeneutically circular activity of using these participants to learn about the emergent rules, but then turning and using those rules to criticize one or another aspect of their play.

I am painfully aware that some readers will remain deeply skeptical, like the bystanders in my story, concluding that there is nothing coherent enough in these gestures for a real game; or that if there is one, it is being played incorrectly; or that perhaps it should not be played at all. Finally, some will be irritated that my players make starkly different ethical-political claims, and yet I don't say much in regard to who, after all, is ultimately right. All I can say in my defense is that my main intention in this book is to give a taste of what good or felicitous play looks like; it is not to declare winners.

ACKNOWLEDGMENTS

Work on the manuscript of this book was greatly facilitated by the hospitality and intellectual life of two universities. I would like to thank Marian Verkerk for inviting me to spend a delightful period as a visiting professor in the summer of 1997, with the Philosophy Faculty at the Erasmus University, Rotterdam; and Axel Honneth and Rainer Forst for hosting me for a wonderful academic year in 1997–98, at the Philosophy Institute of the Goethe University in Frankfurt. The latter stay was made possible by the Alexander von Humboldt Foundation, whose generosity to me over the years has been nothing short of extraordinary.

Thanks are also due to my home university, Virginia Tech, for providing me with a sabbatical; and to the Center for Programs in the Humanities there that, once again, helped fund my work through a Summer Stipend.

I had the opportunity to present portions of the manuscript as papers to various groups: the Political Theory Colloquium, Harvard University; the University for Humanist Studies, Utrecht; the Philosophy Faculty of Erasmus University, Rotterdam; the Philosophy Institute of the Goethe University, Frankfurt; the Postgraduate School of Critical Theory, Nottingham University; the Institute for Cultural Research, Lancaster University; the Olmstead conference, "Instilling Ethics," Yale University; the Political Theory Workshop, the University of Chicago; the Department of Political Science, Duke University; and the Forum for Contemporary Theory, University of Virginia. I would like to thank the participants at those meetings for a multitude of challenging comments and the hosts (Pratap Mehta, Henk Manschot, Marian Verkerk, Axel Honneth, Jon Simons, Michael Dillon, Norma Thompson, Rom Coles, Patchen Markell, Joshua Dienstag, and George Klosko) for their generosity.

An earlier version of portions of chapters 1 and 2 originally appeared as "Weak Ontology and Liberal Political Reflection," *Political Theory* 25 no. 4 (1997): 502–23; portions of chapter 4 originally appeared under the title "As the World Turns: Ontology and Politics in Judith Butler," *Polity* (winter 1999); and portions of chapter 5 originally appeared as " 'Critical Responsiveness' and Justice," symposium on William Connolly's *The Ethos of Pluralization,* in *Philosophy and Social Criticism* 24 no. 1 (1998): 73–81. I appreciate the permission to reprint this material.

I want to express my gratitude to those who read and commented on specific chapters: Jane Bennett, Simon Critchley, Patrick Croskery, Fonna Dubin, Bonnie Honig, Kathy Jones, George Kateb, Tim Luke, Debra

Morris, Scott Roulier, Charles Taylor, and Linda Zerilli. Special thanks go to those who generously found the time to read the full manuscript: Rom Coles, Bill Connolly, Don Moon, and Melissa Orlie. I could make a second career out of trying to do full justice to the perceptive insights generated by their readings.

At Princeton University Press, Ann Himmelberger Wald has been the model of what a good editor should be, as has her successor, Ian Malcolm. As always, the staff of the Department of Political Science at Virginia Tech provided me with crucial support and word-processing skills. I shudder to think how much more difficult the writing process would be without the help and good judgment of Maxine Riley and Kim Hedge.

Pat, Lydia, and Cam make it all worthwhile.

Sustaining Affirmation

INTRODUCTION: THE WEAK ONTOLOGICAL TURN

A CURIOUS COMMONALITY is emerging across a wide variety of contributions in contemporary political theory. Increasingly there is a turn to ontology. This shift might initially seem a little puzzling. For one thing, *ontology* traditionally referred to a fairly restricted field of philosophical reflection concerned with analyzing "being" that was relatively remote from moral-political concerns. What explains the extraordinary expansion of interest? This expansion becomes doubly perplexing when one recalls that ontology was also traditionally closely connected—sometimes even identified—with metaphysics, an activity now regarded by many with deep suspicion.[1]

In trying to understand the recent ontological turn, several contributing factors need to be separated. One is the shift in the meaning of ontology that emerged in the last century in analytic philosophy and philosophy of science. For most English-speaking philosophers, ontology came to refer increasingly to the question of what entities are presupposed by our scientific theories. In affirming a theory, one also takes on a commitment to the existence of certain entities.[2] Ontology in this general sense seems to have been increasingly appropriated in recent years in the social sciences. Thus, one frequently hears reference made to the ontology implicit in some social scientific theory or research tradition.[3]

[1] See the essays on ontology in Hans Burkhardt and Barry Smith, eds., *The Handbook of Metaphysics and Ontology*, vol. 2 (Munich: Philosphia Verlag, 1991). Cf. Alasdair MacIntyre, "Ontology," in *The Encyclopedia of Philosophy* (New York: Macmillan, 1967), 542–43.

[2] W. V. O. Quine, *From a Logical Point of View* (Cambridge: Harvard University Press, 1953); and Larry Laudan, *Progress and Its Problems: Towards a Theory of Scientific Growth* (Berkeley and Los Angeles: University of California Press, 1977), chap. 3.

[3] The notion of ontology likely found its way into the discourse of political science through the methodological discussions of the late 1970s and 1980s. Crucial essays in this regard are J. Donald Moon, "The Logic of Political Inquiry: A Synthesis of Opposed Perspectives," in *Handbook of Political Science*, ed. Fred Greenstein and Nelson Polsby, vol. 1 (Reading, Mass.: Addison-Wesley, 1975); Brian Fay and J. Donald Moon, "What Would an Adequate Philosophy of Social Science Look Like?" *Philosophy of the Social Sciences* 7, no. 3 (1977): 209–27; and Terence Ball, "Is There Progress in Political Science?" in *Idioms of Inquiry: Critique and Renewal in Political Science*, ed. T. Ball (New York: SUNY Press, 1987). The first two essays employed the Lakatosian language of "research programs"; the basic conceptualization of entities within a program was called the "hard core." Ball's essay, under the influence of Larry Laudan's work, explicitly refers to the "ontology" of a "research tradition."

One might think of such usage as a kind of ontological turn in the social sciences, but that is not what I have in mind.

The ontological turn I am referring to emerges with the growing realization that we live in "late modern" times. The sense of living in *late* modernity implies a greater awareness of the conventionality of much of what has been taken for certain in the modern West. The recent ontological shift might then be characterized generally as the result of a growing propensity to interrogate more carefully those "entities" presupposed by our typical ways of seeing and doing in the modern world.

One of the entities most thrown into question has been our conception of the human subject. At issue is the assertive, disengaged self who generates distance from its background (tradition, embodiment) and foreground (external nature, other subjects) in the name of an accelerating mastery of them. This Teflon subject has had a leading role on the modern stage. Such subjectivity has been affirmed primarily at the individual level in Western democracies, although within Marxism it had a career at the collective level as well. In both cases, the relevant entity is envisioned as powering itself through natural and social obstacles; it dreams ultimately of frictionless motion. This modern ontology of the Teflon subject has, of course, not usually been thematized in quite such stark terms. But the lack of explicit thematization has been at least partially a measure of modernity's self-confidence. It is precisely the waning of this self-confidence that engenders such a widespread recourse to ontological reflection. Accordingly, the current turn might now be seen as an attempt to think ourselves, and being in general, in ways that depart from the dominant—but now more problematic—ontological investments of modernity.

Ontological commitments in this sense are thus entangled with questions of identity and history, with how we articulate the meaning of our lives, both individually and collectively. When these aspects of the current turn are brought into the foreground, it quickly becomes apparent how crucial Heidegger is to the story. He brought ontological reflection into a series of entanglements that are central to current thinking. For Heidegger, in *Being and Time,* the analysis of being *(Sein)* cannot be an exclusively cognitive matter, as it was traditionally, and still is, for much of analytic philosophy. It has to be done through an existential analysis of human being *(Dasein).* Ontological reflection thus becomes inextricably entangled with distinctive characteristics of human being, such as mortality and "mood" *(Stimmung).*[4] Further, in his later work, Heidegger gave ontological investigation a historical dimension, insofar as he turned

[4] Martin Heidegger, *Being and Time,* trans. John Macquarrie and Edward Robinson (New York: Harper and Row, 1962).

against the dominant, modern way of understanding human being or subjectivity and indicted the whole tradition of Western metaphysics that, in his view, had sought cognitive frameworks within which to "grasp" being conclusively.[5]

Many who have never read a word of Heidegger have been subjected to his influence through recent French philosophy. His entanglement of ontology with the themes just mentioned has been appropriated and modified in various ways by familiar poststructuralist or postmodern thinkers, such as Foucault, Derrida, and Lyotard.[6] They have helped bring ontological reflection to the forefront of our thought, even though they are in general quite leery of any sustained affirmation of a particular ontology.

However one assesses the role of French philosophy in this regard, it is important to recognize that this stream of thought is only one of several that participate in the current ontological turn. I will be arguing that one finds similar countermodern, ontological themes in various locations across the contemporary intellectual landscape: in communitarianism, in political theory influenced by theology, in feminism, in post-Marxism, and even in some versions of liberalism itself, which is normally seen as being deeply committed to the dominant, modern ontology.[7] In each of these initiatives, ontological concerns emerge in the form of deep reconceptualizations of human being in relation to its world. More specifically, human being is presented as in some way "stickier" than in prevailing modern conceptualizations. Answers vary, of course, as to the character of this stickiness and as to that to which the subject is most prominently stuck. It is important to emphasize this diversity in the ontological turn. When the shift is overidentified with postmodernism, the whole topic is made to appear too dependent upon what is only one manifestation of it; moreover, within that particular current, thinkers have often failed to attend sufficiently to a range of problems related to

[5] See, for example, "What Is Metaphysics?," "Letter on Humanism," and "The Question Concerning Technology," in *Basic Writings,* ed. David Krell (New York: Harper and Row, 1977).

[6] See my discussion of this theme in *Political Theory and Postmodernism* (New York: Cambridge University Press, 1991); and Michael Dillon, "Another Justice," *Political Theory* 27, no. 2 (1999): 155–75.

[7] The following chapters survey work that falls into a number of these categories. A sense of ontological concerns in areas not covered, such as post-Marxism and negative theology, can be gotten from, respectively, Romand Coles's analysis of the work of Ernesto Laclau and Chantal Mouffe in "Liberty, Equality, Receptive Generosity: Neo-Nietzschean Reflections on the Ethics and Politics of Coalition," *American Political Science Review* 90 (June 1996): 375–88; and Aryeh Botwinick, "Maimonides and Hobbes," paper presented at Annual Meeting of the American Political Science Association, Washington, D.C., 1993.

articulating and affirming the very reconceptualizations toward which they gesture.[8]

One might make the case for an ontological turn simply by pointing to evidence of the increasingly frequent use of the term *ontology* in the way I have just elucidated. I am going to push a bit beyond this, however, and argue something stronger and more systematic. Even though one must start by emphasizing the diversity within the ontological turn, one can nevertheless isolate a number of distinctive, common characteristics, in terms of which it is plausible to talk about the emergence of new rules for the game of reflecting upon the most basic conceptualizations of self, other, and world, as well as for how such reflections in turn structure ethical-political thought. There seem to me to be at least four rough characteristics shared by the most perceptive participants in this broad ontological shift. I want to sketch these now in a relatively abstract, introductory fashion. A fuller appreciation of what such characteristics amount to will emerge as they are displayed in the work of the theorists I examine in the various substantive chapters.

1.1. Fundamental *and* Contestable

The first commonality emerges around the question: how is one to understand the epistemological status of such contemporary efforts at *fundamental* conceptualization of human being? Here I want to begin by drawing a distinction between two ideal types of ontology: strong and weak. The late modern ontologies in which I am interested typically exhibit at least some of the characteristics I refer to as "weak," whereas premodern and modern ones have more typically exhibited the characteristics I refer to as "strong."

Strong are those ontologies that claim to show us "the way the world is," or how God's being stands to human being, or what human nature is. It is by reference to this external ground that ethical and political life gain their sense of what is right; moreover, this foundation's validity is unchanging and of universal reach. For strong ontologies, the whole question of passages from ontological truths to moral-political ones is relatively clear. Some proponents do not, of course, assume that political

[8] The overidentification of the ontological drift with postmodernism occludes what may be a useful critical perspective on the latter. In this regard, it can be argued that there is an unconscious tendency in at least some postmodern thinkers to reproduce in a new guise the problem of frictionless subjectivity within their own stance. By this I mean that the affirmed mode of individual agency becomes one of continuous critical motion, incessantly and disruptively unmasking the ways in which the modern subject engenders, marginalizes, and disciplines the others of its background and foreground. The potential, ironic danger here is that the former image of subjectivity comes to look uncomfortably like the latter. Cf. White, *Political Theory and Postmodernism,* 64–65.

principles or decisions can be strictly derived from their ontology; for example, there may be substantial discretionary space for the exercise of judgment. However, in contrast to weak ontologies, strong ones carry an underlying assumption of certainty that guides the whole problem of moving from the ontological level to the moral-political. But this very certainty—both about how things are and how political life should reflect it—allows such ontologies to provide what seem today (at least to some of us) to be answers to our late modern problems that demand too much initial forgetfulness of contingency and indeterminacy. Although terminology is extremely variable here, this last point could be stated thus, that strong ontologies involve too much "metaphysics." Since World War II, there have been a number of prominent proponents of different forms of strong ontology in political theory. Such thinkers as Leo Strauss and Eric Voegelin, as well as adherents to the natural law tradition, have drawn on classical Greek or Christian models in order to contest the dominant modern ontology. Contemporary philosophers like Alasdair MacIntyre have developed novel ways of carrying some of these sorts of arguments forward.[9] But the recent ontological turn that is the primary focus of my attention has taken place largely outside of this immediate sphere of influence. My term *weak ontology* is intended to highlight what is distinctive about this new phenomenon.[10] The thinking I am interested in resists strong ontology, on the one hand, and the strategy of much of liberal thought, on the other. The latter has generally ignored or suppressed ontological reflection, sometimes tacitly affirming the Teflon

[9] Although MacIntyre manifests an admirable willingness to engage alternative perspectives in a sustained and sensitive fashion, and seems to claim that we cannot get beyond the fact of a variety of philosophical traditions, there is behind his reflections a core of absolute certainty when he contrasts his own Catholic tradition with others. He implies that the latter are responsible for, or in complicity with, the "new dark ages"; *After Virtue*, 2d ed. (Notre Dame, Ind.: University of Notre Dame Press, 1984), 245. The deployment of this sort of ultimate metaphor helps convince me that MacIntyre is a strong ontologist in my terms. A useful contrast here might be offered between MacIntyre and Charles Taylor, who also writes within a Catholic tradition, but who, I will argue, is a weak ontologist. For Taylor, our situation is one of a "conversation" between traditions. He can affirm his religious position and offer strong critiques of opponents, but I can't imagine him deploying the metaphor of light and darkness to characterize the relation of his own tradition to that of his opponents. I take up Taylor's views in chapter 3.

For an overview of strong-ontology-based political thought up through the mid-1960s, see Dante Germino, *Beyond Ideology: The Revival of Political Theory* (New York: Harper and Row, 1967).

[10] Gianni Vattimo often employs the term *weak thinking* to gesture in a broadly similar direction; and he has at least once used *weak ontology* synonymously. Although my use of the latter term shares a broad directional emphasis, I have no idea whether Vattimo would find my elucidation of the characteristics of a felicitous weak ontology compatible with his own views. See Vattimo, *The End of Modernity: Nihilism and Hermeneutics in Postmodern Culture*, trans. Jon R. Snyder (Baltimore: Johns Hopkins University Press, 1988), 85–86.

self, sometimes expressing neutrality toward it. Weak ontology finds the costs of such strategies to outweigh the claimed benefits.

One might object that the distinction between strong and weak ontology is merely a relabeling of the familiar distinction between metaphysical and antimetaphysical or postmodern views, or between foundationalist and antifoundationalist ones. This suspicion is true to a degree. But I would claim that this relabeling serves a useful philosophical purpose. My intention in developing the notion of weak ontology is to call greater attention to the kind of interpretive-existential terrain that anyone who places herself in the "anti" position must explore at some point. In short, I want to shift the intellectual burden here from a preoccupation with what is opposed and deconstructed, to an engagement with what must be articulated, cultivated, and affirmed in its wake. My delineation of the characteristics of felicitous, weak ontologies is intended as a contribution toward this goal.

Weak ontologies respond to two pressing concerns. First, there is the acceptance of the idea that all fundamental conceptualizations of self, other, and world are contestable. Second, there is the sense that such conceptualizations are nevertheless necessary or unavoidable for an adequately reflective ethical and political life. The latter insight demands from us the affirmative gesture of constructing foundations, the former prevents us from carrying out this task in a traditional fashion.

One aspect of constructing such contestable foundations involves the embodiment within them of some signaling of their own limits. Felicitous weak ontologies cannot simply declare their contestability, fallibility, or partiality at the start and then proceed pretty much as before. The reason for this is that an ontology figures our most basic sense of human being, an achievement that always carries a propensity toward naturalization, reification, and unity, even if only implicitly. A weak ontology must possess resources for deflecting this propensity at some point in the unfolding of its dimensions. Its elaboration of fundamental meanings must in some sense fold back upon itself, disrupting its own smooth constitution of a unity. In a way, its contestability will thus be enacted rather than just announced.

1.2. A Stickier Subject

I have suggested that one quality evident in the ontological turn is resistance to the "disengaged self."[11] One of the key notions in weak ontology is that of a stickier subject. This notion can take a variety of specific forms,

[11] The term "disengaged self" comes from Charles Taylor, *Sources of the Self: The Making of Modern Identity* (Cambridge, Mass.: Harvard University Press, 1989), 21.

as the following chapters will show, but I want to suggest that within this variety a certain style of argument is apparent. Weak ontologies do not proceed by categorical positings of, say, human nature or telos, accompanied by a crystalline conviction of the truth of that positing. Rather, what they offer are figurations of human being in terms of certain existential realities, most notably language, mortality or finitude, natality, and the articulation of "sources of the self."[12] These figurations are accounts of what it is *to be* a certain sort of creature: first, one entangled with language; second, one with a consciousness that it will die; third, one that, despite its entanglement and limitedness, has the capacity for radical novelty; and, finally, one that gives definition to itself against some ultimate background or "source," to which we find ourselves always already attached, and which evokes something like awe, wonder, or reverence. This sense of a background that can be both empowering and humbling is *mis*construed when grasped either as something with a truth that reveals itself to us in an unmediated way or as something that is simply a matter of radical choice. I am borrowing the notion of sources from Charles Taylor, whose work is taken up in chapter 3. While this might appear to give the idea of weak ontology a necessarily theistic cast from the start, since Taylor is indeed a theist, such a conclusion would be incorrect. Perhaps the simplest way to demonstrate the philosophical richness of Taylor's notion of sources is to show how it helps in the interpretation of nontheistic thinkers, something I will try to do throughout the book.

When I speak of "existential realities," I mean to claim that language, finitude, natality, and sources are in some brute sense universal constitutives of human being, but also that their meaning is irreparably underdetermined in any categorical sense. There is, for example, simply no demonstrable essence of language or true meaning of finitude. Weak ontologies offer figurations of these universals, whose persuasiveness can never be fully disentangled from an interpretation of present historical circumstances. Fundamental conceptualization here thus means acknowledging that gaining access to something universal about human being and world is always also a construction that cannot rid itself of a historical dimension.

For weak ontology, human being is the negotiation of these existential realities. But when this negotiation is imagined in the fashion of a Teflon self powering itself through the world, there has been an unacceptable impoverishment of figuration. Accepting such an image implies, for example, a figuration of language as, in essence, an instrument: in effect we always "have" language; it never "has" us. Of course, as I just empha-

[12] Ibid.

sized, such a claim of impoverishment can never be disentangled from historical claims; in this case, claims regarding, say, the various "costs" that Western modernity has had to pay for such a tight embrace of the disengaged self.

So it is through their renewed figuration of these existential universals that weak ontologies compose portraits of human being that are "stickier"; ones, for example, that are more attuned to how language "has" us, and more attentive to vivifying our finitude.

Even though I have emphasized that existential universals are radically underdetermined, one might well wonder how I picked out just these four candidates for such an exalted position in the project of weak ontology. My only answer here is that I find that an engagement with both the traditional problems of moral-political philosophy and the specific questions of late modernity is persuasive only if at least these four existential universals are brought to bear. No claim is implied that others may not be shown to be similarly significant. The appropriate way to test the validity of my initial selection of four is simply to see for oneself whether I am persuasive in my attempts to show how particular thinkers encounter significant problems when they neglect one or more of these universals.

1.3. Cultivation

To speak of "portraits" of human being and "figuration" is to begin calling attention to another characteristic of weak ontologies. They are not simply cognitive in their constitution and effects, but also aesthetic-affective. They not only reflect something that is the case about the reality of human being, but also engender a certain sensibility toward that reality. They disclose the world to us in such a way that we think *and* feel it differently than we might otherwise. Their appeal turns partially on how well they allow us to cope with the pressures and challenges of late modern life.

Weak ontologies have an aesthetic-affective quality in another way as well. This relates to the issue of embracing or adopting them. Since such ontologies do not reflect clear, crystalline truth about the world, they do not entice us with any knockdown power to convince or convert. Within the ontological turn the notion of "cultivation" is continually evoked. The embrace of a weak ontology has a tentative, experimental aspect; one must patiently bring it to life by working it into one's life. In this sense, it is at least somewhat different from conversion (on some accounts) to a religious faith or the rational conviction that such and such is the categorically correct moral rule or code. Yet this emphasis on tentativeness does not imply that one's relation to an ontology is like that to a suit of new clothes taken home on approval. The cognitive and affective burdens entailed in revisioning the world ensure that when one seriously embraces an ontology, one does not do so in a "light and transient" way. The process of adoption is the initiation of a process of cultivation of oneself and one's disposition to the world. This cultivation unfolds through the measured pursuit of an array of related practices and self-disciplines.

In this sense, weak ontologies share similarities with traditional notions of cultivating virtues. But in the case of the latter, the framework of truth, or the telos, within which the virtues acquire their significance is the unshakable foundation on the basis of which the cultivation proceeds. Such is not the case with weak ontologies. The framework itself is never fully immune from the work of cultivation. Pressures for reconceptualizing or further articulating aspects of it continually arise in the ongoing activity of making specific ethical and political judgments and constructing historical interpretations of who "we" are.

1.4. Circuits of Reflection, Affect, and Argumentation

How precisely do weak ontologies constitute a "foundation" of ethical-political life? Since such ontologies can make no strong claim to reflect the pure truth of being, one cannot derive any clear and incontestable principles or values for ethics and politics. The fundamental conceptualizations such an ontology provides can, at most, prefigure practical insight or judgment, in the sense of providing broad cognitive and affective orientation. Practice draws sustenance from an ontology in the sense of both a reflective bearing upon possibilities for action and a mobilizing of motivational force.

If a critic presses for justification of a particular action or norm adopted in light of a weak ontology, the appropriate response is not a simple and conclusive recourse to the "foundation." Vertical, one-way images of justification are misleading here (whether the path of justification is imagined as leading up to a skyhook or down to a foundation). An ontology certainly articulates our most fundamental intimations of human being, but it is best to think of such intimation as always part of a horizontal circuit of reflection, affect, and argumentation. The circuit is a three-cornered one, with critical energy and discrimination flowing back and forth to each corner. One corner is formed by the judgments and norms relevant to specific contexts of action; these, as I have said, receive a prefiguring influence from ontological concepts, which in turn constitute a second corner. But, as I also noted, such concepts are themselves not immune from pressures for revision arising out of insights gleaned from specific action contexts.

And these two corners are in a similar, two-way relation with the third corner, which is constituted by one's broadest historical "we" claims and narratives.[13] Think for a moment about Lyotard's well-known notion that the "grand narratives" or "metanarratives" (focused around God, Nature, or Progress) of the modern West have increasingly lost their power to convince.[14] He extols instead a proliferation of "petits récits," or "small narratives," for our postmodern times. But perhaps this dichotomy is somewhat misleading. Lyotard is right in his critique of generalizing narratives fixed upon an unshakable philosophical foundation. But the simple image of proliferating small narratives neglects the unavoidable pressures toward generalization in a world where my or our narrative sooner or later runs up against yours. As Clifford Geertz has so nicely put it, "now . . . nobody is leaving anybody alone and isn't ever again going to."[15] What sort of engagement there will be between one small narrative and another only takes shape within the construction, however implicit, of a "grand" or at least grander narrative.

My delineation of the foregoing characteristics of a weak ontology constitutes both a *description* of what I find in the most admirable contributions to the ontological turn, as well as the beginnings of *loose criteria* for assessing the felicity of any given contribution. Whether these criteria are ultimately plausible or illuminating in the way they would have one think about contemporary ethics and political thought is a question best unpacked in the course of considering whether the readings I offer in the following chapters stand up or not. The theorists whose work I examine were chosen both because I find them to be perceptive and distinctive and because they cover a broad spectrum of contemporary views. Again, my underlying aim is to display the phenomenon of weak ontology in an unexpected variety of philosophical quarters. I round up the *un*usual suspects.

I start in chapter 2 in a quarter that has generally been quite skeptical of ontological reflection, namely, liberalism. An interesting initiative

[13] Having drawn this picture of a circuit of justification, it should be clear where I stand in regard to philosophers who claim that either ontology or ethics is *the* proper starting point of philosophical reflection. Emmanuel Levinas, for example, famously critiques Heidegger for making ontology the first philosophy, whereas in reality it should be ethics; *Totality and Infinity: An Essay on Exteriority*, trans. A. Lingis (Pittsburgh: Duquesne University Press, 1969). My thought is that there simply is no privileged starting place. Ontological figurations will always be expressing ethical concerns to a degree and ethical insights will always be rooted in some specific way of conceptually carving up self, other, and world.

[14] Jean-François Lyotard, *The Postmodern Condition: A Report on Knowledge*, trans. G. Bennington and B. Massumi (Minneapolis: University of Minnesota Press, 1984), xxiv.

[15] Clifford Geertz, "Local Knowledge: Fact and Law in Comparative Perspective," in *Local Knowledge* (New York: Basic Books, 1983), 234.

here is George Kateb's attempt to rethink the foundations of liberalism in such a way as to overcome some of the drawbacks that the dominant modern ontology has embedded in that philosophy. By constructing a novel ontological basis, he would relieve liberalism of the familiar charge that it is intrinsically tied to a picture of selves as "monads" or "possessive individualists" whose essential connection to others is constituted instrumentally in terms of self-interest. Since Kateb is speaking from within the liberal tradition, it is perhaps unsurprising that he does not explicitly have much recourse to the language of ontology to describe what he is doing. But that does not really bother me; I am less interested in explicit terminology than in whether ontological refiguration of a certain sort is in fact occurring, and how it is related to ethical-political judgments.

Charles Taylor's work is the focus of chapter 3. His critique of procedural liberalism and affirmation of a kind of communitarianism is certainly self-consciously carried out with explicit ontological claims. *That* he thinks ontologically is thus less of an issue than *how.* Most critics see him as employing a variant of theistically rooted, strong ontology. I will dissent from that judgment, arguing that Taylor in fact provides a fascinating illustration of how theism of a certain kind can frame itself in weak ontological terms.

In chapter 4, I turn to the writings of Judith Butler. Her work is clearly associated with ontology, but primarily in a negative way. Her efforts to find bearings for feminism and gay and lesbian thought have proceeded by means of a persistent critique of the way ontology has traditionally worked to dissimulate power by installing in ethical-political views a level of conceptualization that is beyond contestation. But, as Butler has pursued this line of thought, an affirmative ontological gesture of her own has increasingly become apparent. Like many other poststructuralist or postmodern thinkers, her suspicion of traditional ontology seems to produce some unwillingness to thematize explicitly the philosophical implications of her own gesture. Nevertheless, that gesture is a bold one, possessing more felicity than her critics might lead one to think.

Finally, I turn to perhaps the most conscious contemporary articulator of weak ontology, William Connolly. Like Butler's, his views are broadly describable as poststructuralist or postmodern, although unlike her, his early intellectual roots are not in continental philosophy, but rather in Anglo-American political theory.[16] He is also unlike many poststructuralists or postmodernists in that he is never troubled by bouts of austerity when it comes to the necessity of affirming the weak ontological task. It is the conscious balance he maintains between the critical activity of

[16] See, for example, *The Terms of Political Discourse,* 2d ed. (Princeton, N.J.: Princeton University Press, 1983). The first edition of this book was published in 1974.

genealogy, in the Nietzschean and Foucauldian sense, on the one hand, and the affirmative activity of articulating an ontology, on the other, that makes his work especially challenging.

Before turning to the substantive analysis, a few cautions and clarifications must be issued. Some readers, especially those trained as professional philosophers, will object from the start that I am simply misusing the concept of ontology, expanding and distorting it. Ontology should refer only to the study of the question: What is being? And ontology is intrinsically concerned with a *true* answer to this single question.[17] Accordingly, it could be argued that the way I bring the theme of contestability into play, as well as the way I expand the range of topics with which ontology is entangled, together contribute to making a complete hash of the concept.

In my defense, I would start by again pointing out that a wide variety of thinkers today are using the concept of ontology in a fashion at least somewhat similar to mine. That is the point of my having started by referring to an ontological turn today. I think the authors whose work I take up might reject one or another aspect of my reading of them, but I doubt they would find my deployment of the concept of ontology to be entirely obtuse.

At this point, the critic could of course take refuge in the objection that the *widespread* misuse of a concept is nevertheless still misuse. But if we think about conceptual change, it is often the case that new uses of a concept are initially identified and criticized as misuses. Think, for example, of the way the usage of the notion of natural right began to shift in the seventeenth century away from an almost exclusive connotation of a right direction for subjects to the additional notion of something that the individual in some sense possessed. Or think of how democracy, over the course of the nineteenth and twentieth centuries, lost its original negative connotations of disorder and acquired what are now almost exclusively positive connotations. One can easily imagine how defenders of traditional views would have accused their opponents of gross conceptual confusion.

But if weak ontology is thus not entirely confused in a conceptual sense, then perhaps it will be nevertheless so thin in its claims as to amount to nothing more finally than a good helping of air sauce and wind pudding. As for "thinness," I hope that the following chapters, especially the one on Butler, will make clear that weakness and thinness are not the same thing; a felicitous weak ontology should be a rich one, in

[17] Some of these questions were pressed on me by Simon Critchley in a set of very thoughtful comments on a paper I presented at the Annual Meeting of the American Political Science Association, Washington D.C., September 1997.

terms of the array of concepts it deploys and the skill with which they are elaborated. Furthermore, the affirmation of a weak ontology should not be confused with a stance of continual indecisiveness. I have no doubt that in the nineteenth century many found J. S. Mill's treatment of the uncertainty of practical truth claims in *On Liberty* to imply a paralyzing abandonment of healthy certitudes. But liberals today who make a virtue of Mill's uncertainty don't seem particularly eaten up with paralysis and confusion. Similarly, I see no reason for thinking that acceptance of the central ideas of weak ontology will necessarily imply any debilitating weakness in the practice of one's life. In fact, I would suggest they are more likely to foster a kind of ethical strength. Again, think of Mill. Certainly he was giving up a kind of strength in his claims, but he turned the tables on his opponents. A strength born of an unwarranted rejection of contingency is its own kind of atrophy: a moral-intellectual couch-potatoism that stands in contrast to the active qualities he associated with true "individuality."[18] Similarly, if I am right about weak ontology, it affirms the need for an even greater ethical "fitness," something that is thematized in its particular emphasis on cultivation. One cultivates and contests at more levels of life than the Millean individual.

Another set of criticisms would likely emerge from the position occupied by Richard Rorty. For him, a notion like weak ontology is just a philosophically stilted way of saying "my perspective" on certain topics. Once we give up on strong ontology with its straightforward truth claims, there is just "my perspective," of which one can merely say that it is more or less useful for my "private purposes" of "self-creation."[19] This complaint embodies two sorts of skepticism about weak ontology. The first involves reason and criteria; the second, the relation of philosophical reflection to the private and public spheres.

As for the first sort of skepticism, I understand the Rortyean complaint to be that in a postmetaphysical world, there is just my view and your view, and we should be very careful about dressing up one or the other with any philosophical language that might imply some metaphysical truth claims. In one sense, there is something perpetually refreshing about Rorty's challenge here; it is a good kind of stock criticism to turn upon oneself from time to time. In another sense, however, this complaint, if it is merely repeated like a slogan, begins to have a rather stale smell. My efforts in this book are directed toward looking a bit more

[18] John Stuart Mill, "On Liberty," in *On Liberty and Other Writings*, ed. Stefan Collini (Cambridge: Cambridge University Press, 1989), 59.

[19] Richard Rorty, "Remarks on Deconstruction and Pragmatism," in *Deconstruction and Pragmatism*, ed. Simon Critchley (London: Routledge, 1996), 16–17. Cf. *Contingency, Irony, Solidarity* (Cambridge: Cambridge University Press, 1989).

closely at what makes a set of ideas about fundamental things relatively persuasive today. In effect, it is an exploration of some middle terrain between strong ontology and bald assertions of *my* perspective. My hope is that some possibly interesting things might be said here. The implication of Rorty's complaint is rather that all such efforts are necessarily somehow doomed at the start.

But why should we be so quick to embrace the bipolar world from which this confident judgment flows? Does the simple option of either affirming a strong ontology or proclaiming my perspective not betray a curiously insistent desire to shut off speculation and careful reflection about things in the middle? The real question is: Do the sorts of considerations I draw together in my explication of weak ontology help us think more creatively about the tasks of contemporary moral and political theory or not?

Here we come to Rorty's second ground for skepticism. He finds not the slightest reason to expect that muddling around with notions like weak ontology will produce any legitimate insight for public life. At most it can enhance our efforts at private self-creation. A failure to grasp this truth, moreover, can constitute a real danger to the public world of "real politics," which needs to be discussed only in "banal, familiar terms—terms that do not need philosophical dissection and do not have philosophical presuppositions."[20] As many of his critics have pointed out, the persuasiveness of Rorty's claims here rests on the persuasiveness of his account of public and private. But he has never done more than deploy this distinction in a very general, rhetorical fashion. This deployment has typically been directed at those poststructuralist and postmodernist critics of liberal political institutions whose attacks are long on hyperbole and corrosive language, but short on affirmative conceptualization of, and orientation to, concrete practices and institutions. In effect, Rorty is meeting bludgeon with bludgeon. Within the range of postmodern and poststructuralist critiques of liberalism and modernity, there are some that definitely fit Rorty's portrait. But if my hunch in this book is correct, there is now increasing attention being paid, both within that critical current, as well as others, to the question of affirmation broadly and to the issue of how ontological figures structure ethical-political insight in specific ways. If this is true, then perhaps Rorty's bludgeoning tactics begin to look a bit dated. In the present contest, only thugs would continue to use it.

Since Rorty is not a thug, he will now have to give a more careful account of his sharp distinction between public and private. And I suspect that will be more difficult than he imagines, at least if he is going to

[20] Rorty, "Remarks."

try to continue to strictly quarantine so much reflection and speculation within the private sphere. If this is true, then there seems to be as much of a burden of proof on the Rortyean as on the weak ontologist. Moreover, at one point, Rorty even admits that the sort of speculations included within weak ontology may have at least some public effect. They may, he concedes, be "politically consequential, [but only] in a very indirect and long-term way."[21] When one combines Rorty's own unclarity about the public-private distinction with this admission, and one allows for reasonable disputes over how "indirect" and how "long-term," I would suggest that a good bit of running room opens up for the project upon which this book embarks.

But at least some of Rorty's suspicions about ontology might be given more life if they were seen as concerns shared by liberals generally. Accordingly, one variant of liberalism admits ontology, but only on its terms, arguing that political theory needs only one ontological source: the autonomous, disengaged self. Anything more is dangerous. Another variant—"political liberalism"—argues that the justness of the neutral, liberal state can be established without any recourse whatsoever to ontological sources.[22] The chapters on Taylor and Connolly will contest both of these lines of argument.

[21] Ibid.

[22] For the concept of "political liberalism," see John Rawls, *Political Liberalism* (New York: Columbia University Press, 1993); Donald Moon, *Constructing Community: Moral Pluralism and Tragic Conflicts* (Princeton, N.J.: Princeton University Press, 1993); Charles Larmore, *The Morals of Modernity* (Cambridge: Cambridge University Press, 1996); and Rorty, "The Priority of Democracy," in *The Virginia Statutes of Religious Freedom,* ed. M. Peterson and R. Vaughan (Cambridge: Cambridge University Press, 1988).

Chapter Two

ONTOLOGICAL UNDERCURRENTS WITHIN LIBERALISM: GEORGE KATEB'S "DEMOCRATIC INDIVIDUALITY"

GEORGE KATEB is a staunch liberal. He affirms unequivocally the absolute supremacy of individual rights over all other values. He extols John Rawls's *A Theory of Justice* as "the great statement of individualism in this century."[1] Moreover, representative democracy is categorically—not just pragmatically—preferred by Kateb to direct democracy, since the latter always threatens rights. He is almost constitutionally averse to any moral-political claims advanced on behalf of ideas of community, active citizenship, religion, or group identity. Kateb does not mince words. Communitarianism, for example, has "too many affinities to fascism." Similarly, the "normal condition" of group identity is "derangement."[2]

Despite Kateb's initial appearance as a fully confident liberal, he is nevertheless somewhat anxious. At the core of this anxiety is the worry that, within mainstream liberalism, "individualism is not always seen in its fullness."[3] A remedy for this deficiency can be had, however, by drawing upon a particular strand of American thought; specifically, the "Emersonian tradition," which includes Ralph Waldo Emerson, Henry David Thoreau, and Walt Whitman. At the heart of their work is the concept of "democratic individuality." "The Emersonian tradition is an attempt to sever democratic individuality from all other individualisms that resemble but reject or betray it, or that developed with it but then swerve and become narrowly extreme." The worst of these "other individualisms" are those that conceive the self as either a "possessive individualist," where others and the world come into focus only in light of self-interest

The following abbreviations will be used for referring to Kateb's books:

ESR *Emerson and Self-Reliance.* Thousand Oaks, Calif.: Sage Publications, 1995.

HA *Hannah Arendt: Politics, Conscience, Evil.* Totowa, N.J.: Roman and Alanheld, 1983.

IO *The Inner Ocean: Individualism and Democratic Culture.* Ithaca, N.Y.: Cornell University Press, 1992.

[1] "Democratic Individuality and the Meaning of Rights," in *Liberalism and the Moral Life,* ed. N. Rosenblum (Cambridge: Harvard University Press, 1989), 184.

[2] *IO,* 213, 229.

[3] "Democratic Individuality," 185.

and instrumental use; or as simply "monadic," implying a self-sufficient subject that surveys others in a radically detached fashion, always in methodical control of any terms of engagement.[4] When liberalism gets too closely associated with such conceptions, it becomes easier prey for its critics.

Thus, the critic might assert that Rawls, for example, operates to some degree (at least in *A Theory of Justice*) with a disengaged conception of the self: a creature whose orientation to the moral-political world is conceived in crucial ways as one of detached cognition and calculation. Kateb is extremely careful here. He never wants to admit directly that such criticism hits home, and thus that mainstream liberalism really needs much in the way of help from the Emersonians. At one point, he goes so far as to say that liberalism's defenders "have ample resources at their disposal to fend off the critics, without having to enlist the Emersonians." This makes it sound as though Kateb's elaboration of democratic individuality is merely an amusing sideshow in the main arena of liberalism; interesting perhaps, but not crucial to the success of the show as a whole. But Kateb's own practice makes one highly suspicious of such a disavowal. He is not an intellectual historian concerned with merely portraying a fascinating episode in American thought. He is a moralist and political thinker with a mission to which he is passionately committed: "the renovation of liberalism." This mission's aim is to show that the "deeper meaning" of liberalism's commitment to rights lies in the idea of democratic individuality, with its distinctive way of thinking self, other, and world; in fact, the realization of this idea "is what democracy is for."[5]

The power of what the Emersonian tradition has left us resides in a way of conceiving human being that gives an adequate rendering of both the separateness of the self and its constitutive "connectedness" with others and the world.[6] It is the latter aspect, of course, that distinguishes the ontology underlying democratic individuality from the ones underlying the sort of flawed individualisms just mentioned. Thus, in relation to the ontological turn I have sketched, Kateb's thought holds out the promise that the core ideas of the liberal tradition can be defended in a way that clearly cuts that tradition loose from any necessary connection with ontologies of the disengaged self.[7]

Such a departure immediately entangles Kateb with one dimension of weak ontological reflection. In what follows, I want to show how this

[4] *IO,* 28, 96–97.

[5] "Democratic Individuality," 186, 190; *IO,* 27, 80, 96, 258.

[6] *IO,* 241–42, 245–47, 256.

[7] For a critic of Kateb who has noticed the rich ontological quality of his insights, see Nancy Rosenblum's very interesting essay "Strange Attractors: How Individualists Connect to Form Democratic Unity," *Political Theory* 18 no. 4 (1990): 578.

entanglement opens as well into several other dimensions. In short, his thinking displays a number of the characteristics of a felicitous weak ontology (section 2.1). After drawing out this general affinity, as well as some significant disaffinities, I turn to the issue of how his conception of human being orients Kateb's ethical-political insight. In a broad sense, this orientation does indeed follow the pattern I call prefiguration, which is appropriate for weak ontology. Nevertheless, I will argue that there are some difficulties with the adequacy of the connections Kateb sketches between his ontological figures and the specific moral and political judgments he makes (section 2.2).

2.1. The Ontology of Democratic Individuality

What is striking about Kateb's renovation of liberalism is not just his recourse to ontological reflection, but also the way his figurations are bound up with the idea of aesthetic-affective cultivation. It is to the elaboration of these themes that I will turn first (section 2.1.A). As he draws upon the Emersonians to construct his ideal of democratic individuality, Kateb is nevertheless aware that this ideal is finally indebted to a subtle but persistent religious sense of wholeness and reconciliation that provides too certain a guarantee to the ontology. He feels therefore the need to put what I call a fold into this ontology, a turning back of conceptualization and affect upon that animating sense of divine coherence (section 2.1.B).

2.1.A. The Inner Ocean and Democratic Aestheticism

For Kateb, an adequate defense of liberalism must start not with an ahistorical, hypothetical reasoning process, as Rawls did in *A Theory of Justice,* but rather within a grand narrative of modern democracy, especially as it emerged in the United States. The ontology of democratic individuality is, accordingly, to be understood as an elucidation of "the deep meanings of living in a rights-based democracy."[8] But the rooting of fundamental concepts in a historical context is, by itself, hardly enough to qualify Kateb as a weak ontologist. Rawls himself in his recent work has, of course, admitted the historical embeddedness of his account of justice, even if he has continued to think that ontological reflection is unnecessary to it.[9] The distinctiveness of Kateb's direction emerges, however, when he contends that among the many important meaning complexes upon which liberal democratic politics rests, the most crucial one for

[8] *IO,* 7, 258.

[9] John Rawls, *Political Liberalism* (New York: Columbia University Press, 1993).

him is a certain feeling, "a sentiment." With the emergence of modern democracy, a distinctive feeling began to throw down historical roots: "that every individual is equally a world, an infinity, a being who is irreplaceable." It is only within the sway of this sentiment that one can grasp *both* the separateness and connectedness that are intrinsic to the notion of equal human dignity: the separateness that constitutes the "existential significance of rights" and the connectedness that binds all persons in a democracy.[10] Such a sentiment is first vivified fully only within the ontology offered by the Emersonians.

It might be objected at this point that Kateb's sentiment of individual infinity actually makes its appearance in the West with Christianity, not with modern democracy. In some broad sense, Kateb would probably not dispute this, but he would insist that a distinctive, *secular* sense of each as an "inner ocean" appears only in the nineteenth century. The ontology of the Emersonians provides us with a portrait of "a new relation to reality," a different way of comprehending self, other, and world that starts to break with the requirement of a God. Kateb is, of course, amply aware of a religious dimension in these thinkers, but he is convinced that their ontology can be freed from this investment without any essential distortion. Such an effort at extrication "simply continue[s] the process of secularization of theological and metaphysical insight that the Emersonians did so much to advance."[11]

Although Kateb draws upon all three of the Emersonians to compose the notion of democratic individuality, it is Whitman that seems to express the core ideas most simply and forcefully. He is "perhaps the greatest philosopher of the culture of democracy."[12] From his work, we can extract the primitive concepts of a distinctive ontology. The "key term" is *soul,* especially as it occurs in the poem "Song of Myself." The soul, in the secular sense that Kateb wants to isolate, is

> What is given in the person, and in all persons the given is the same: the same desires, inclinations, and passions as well as aptitudes and incipient talents. The secular soul is made up of the unwilled, the unbidden, the dreamt, the inchoate and unshaped. It is the reservoir of potentialities. Its roots are wordless. It exists to be observed and worked on, to be realized.[13]

The soul in this secular sense is not divorced from the body; indeed, "There is little point to the contrast."[14]

[10] *IO,* 5, 241.

[11] "Democratic Individuality," 195.

[12] *IO,* 93–96, 240. Kateb refers to Emerson as "the founder of the philosophy of democratic individuality" (*ESR,* 197).

[13] *IO,* 91, 245.

[14] *IO,* 245. For the idea of a secular soul in Emerson, see *ESR,* 86.

The soul then is a reservoir, an "inner ocean," of "infinite potentialities." Only a tiny number of these are actually brought to realization at any given time; and the content of that specific actualization is one's "personality." The entity that does this work of realization is the "self." It constructs a definite social persona from the "indefinite multiplicity" of the soul; in short, it constructs an individual.[15]

In our ordinary social intercourse, we tend to think of personality in reified terms, both in our own case and in that of others. We speak and interact across a divide of apparently fixed individual differences and divergent projects. This is, in effect, the world of disconnected, individual selves imagined by the dominant modern ontology. Kateb's Whitman wants us to see how cramped and partial a picture of human being this actually is. Toward this goal, he draws our attention to a second sort of work the self can engage in, in order to overcome such a narrowness of understanding. In addition to its normal job of fashioning and sustaining a personality, the self can also generate distance from this workaday world and observe, as it were, the whole complex of its activity. What is striking from this detached perspective is, first, the disparity between the narrowness of my actualized personality and the infinite potentiality of the soul. Second, others now appear to me not primarily as fixed crystallizations of difference, but as particular personalities partially submerged in an ocean of potentiality. And when they are seen in this light, I come to understand that the specific character they have actualized out of that reservoir could just as well have been one *I* realized: "I am potentially all personalities and we equally are infinite potentialities."[16] This is the sense Kateb wants to give to the many instances in Whitman's "Song of Myself" where boundaries of identity are blurred or dissolved. Undoubtedly, the most famous line in this regard is "every atom belonging to me as good belongs to you."[17]

This entanglement of particularity and infinitude constitutes one of Kateb's deepest ontological sources. It constitutes the terms within which he thematizes both connectedness and natality. As for the former, when one comprehends being in these terms, one has grasped human connectedness in a way that accords an equal recognition to all others. Each is a particular disclosure of that shared "inner ocean" or soul. To admit both this "compositeness and ultimate unknowability is to open oneself to a kinship to others . . . [a] mutuality of strangers." Natality is brought into ontological focus as that irruptive moment of particular or individ-

[15] *IO,* 244–46.

[16] *IO,* 244–46.

[17] Quoted in *IO,* 244.

ual disclosure out of an infinitude of possibilities. For Kateb, it is attentiveness to the spectacle of this disclosive moment that is at the heart of the Emersonian praise of individualism. In the peculiar interplay between this moment of particularity and the "residual and inexhaustible potentiality" out of which it emerges, we experience profound awe and "reverence" for being.[18]

The affirmation of such an ontology is not well comprehended on the model of a clear-cut, discrete shift from one belief to another or from adherence to one moral principle to another. Within weak ontology, a new cognitive orientation is intimately and continually entangled with the aesthetic-affective activity of cultivation. For Kateb, Whitman's work bears eloquent testimony to this insight. We bring the primitive figurations of connectedness and equal recognition to life only by consistently cultivating an ethos of "democratic aestheticism."[19] Such an ethos aims at engendering attitudes and feelings that allow us to see the multiplicity and contrariety of the world as beautiful, and thereby "to receive all things in the world as equal." The "decisive effect" of democratic aestheticism then is to entice us "to enlarge the imagination of morality."[20]

At this point it is worth emphasizing that the ontology of the disengaged self, as it has appeared in liberal thought, has often been linked with a suspicion of, or outright hostility to, views that look to open the moral-political dimension to the effects of aesthetic-affective experience. The "aestheticization" of politics has been linked with a variety of antiliberal political ideologies, especially fascism.[21] Clearly, the disengaged self has been most at home in the medium of cognition and the limited family of affects associated with exchange relations.[22]

Such strategies, by which the aesthetic-affective dimension is held at a distance or radically truncated, are actively resisted within the ontological turn. Kateb, as a resolute liberal, is obviously aware of the dangers of aestheticism; but he is also convinced that aestheticism is "inescapable." Further, "It may, more than anything else, provide interest in life, its

[18] *IO,* 252–54; *ESR,* 8–9. Kateb is, of course, aware of how Hannah Arendt used the concept of natality. He resists her privileging of the specific natality of political action, preferring instead an Emersonian reading that sees natality in "human struggle against limitation" (*HA,* 163, 171–83).

[19] "Democratic Individuality," 197. This idea is developed at length in "Aestheticism and Morality: Their Cooperation and Hostility," *Political Theory* 28 no. 1 (2000).

[20] "Aestheticism and Morality," 34.

[21] Cf. See Jane Bennett, " 'How Is It, Then, That We Still Remain Barbarians?' Foucault, Schiller, and the Aestheticization of Ethics," *Political Theory* 23 no. 4 (1996).

[22] Cf. Albert Hirschman, *The Passions and the Interests: Political Arguments for Capitalism before Its Triumph* (Princeton, N.J.: Princeton University Press, 1977), part 1.

motion and animation."[23] We are creatures with what Kateb calls "aesthetic cravings," by which he means something close to Samuel Johnson's idea of a "hunger of the imagination which preys incessantly upon life, and must be appeased by some employment."[24]

What exactly are such cravings and by what "employment" are they best appeased? Aesthetic cravings can take many forms, but at their core they bear testimony to the way we desperately insist that existence, as it is or as it might be, yield up to us a face that is beautiful or sublime; a face that is pure, has form or coherence, is striking or colorful, awe-inspiring, mysterious, and so on. We crave, then, that the world have, one way or the other, "a certain sort of meaning or meaningfulness, and at just about any cost (in morality or, we can add, truth)." Only such meaning can satisfy the hunger of the imagination.[25]

Kateb invites us to reconceive many of the familiar motivations of social and political life in terms of aesthetic cravings *that are not acknowledged as such.* Unconscious aestheticism is, he thinks, at the heart of much of what has always powered political life: claims and ideals relating to religion, culture, group identity, masculinity, and "assertive or self-expressive individualism," to name a few. The failure to recognize the aestheticism at the core of each of these enhances immensely their propensity to propagate evil while maintaining innocence.

If, as Kateb says, aestheticism in some form is inescapable, then the real issue becomes how to live with it; more specifically, how to "respond to social reality aesthetically and yet not immorally." This task requires, first, acknowledging our aesthetic insistences; and, second, disciplining and cultivating them so that cravings become transformed into "aesthetic attitudes and feelings."[26] By this, Kateb means that we must try to cultivate the attitudes and feelings typically associated with the reception of, and response to, artworks, only now we try to bring them to bear upon social reality. Which attitudes and feelings?

> Aesthetic *attitudes* are perception, observation, and contemplation; noticing and watching; staring and looking hard; studying and waiting; taking things in and letting nothing be lost; staying with the thing or condition, dwelling with or near it; caring about it while letting it be; and so on. These attitudes arouse or are aroused by essentially aesthetic *feelings:* appreciation, admiration, sometimes wonder or amazement or astonishment.[27]

[23] "Aestheticism and Morality," 30.

[24] Ibid., 12–14. The quotation from Johnson is from *Rasselas,* chap. 32.

[25] "Aestheticism and Morality," 14.

[26] Ibid., 20, 22.

[27] Ibid., 21.

Furthermore, such orientations are usually understood to involve some "distance or detachment," or, following Kant, disinterest. One responds properly to art when its "works are allowed to be external to oneself and to affect oneself on their own terms. There is no desire to make them over." Through the cultivation of such a bearing in relation to social reality, we can "school ourselves in the mitigation of aesthetic cravings."[28] In effect, the best appeasement of such cravings lies in self-disciplines that break up and disperse their momentum.

There are no guarantees. Kateb is aware that the affirmation of fascism can come not just in the uncultivated, emotional form best typified by Nazism, but also in a detached, cultivated form, visible in the admiration of Italian fascism of the 1920s and 1930s, expressed by such figures as W. B. Yeats, Ezra Pound, and Wyndham Lewis.[29] But directions such as these are made more unlikely by democratic aestheticism, since its objects are never collective. Within the ontology of souls, the only human objects toward which aesthetic attitudes are appropriate are individuals. We cultivate a sense of the beauty of particulars only after "breaking the world up into individuals."[30]

It is this peculiar combination of moral and aesthetic sensibility for which Whitman provides the unequaled example. In "Song of Myself" especially, we see the consummate effort to "make democratic poetical understanding."[31] This means learning to bring to life our connectedness through the "poet's virtues of receptivity." Such an exploration gives force to the insight that, because of the identity of "souls," your actual "personality" and action are as much possible realizations of *my* potentiality as they are of yours. Everyone and everything are thus equally deserving of careful attentiveness. In giving this attention, this recognition, "one is only doing justice to *oneself,* to one's composite nature."[32]

Democratic aestheticism is always straining to "bestow the various aesthetic attitudes of appreciation, admiration, wonder (and so on) on everything indiscriminately." This effort to feel our connectedness through seeing beauty in others, even where at first nothing attractive or engaging appears, draws upon our capacity to project ourselves sympathetically or empathetically into others, "to connect to others by identifying with them."[33] As Whitman audaciously imagines,

[28] Ibid.

[29] Ibid., 19–20, 27–28.

[30] *IO,* 34

[31] *IO,* 246; *HA,* 180–181. Kateb notes that Whitman had some other ways of thinking about the relation of aesthetics and society; "Aestheticism and Morality," 24.

[32] *IO,* 253.

[33] *IO,* 246, 249; "Aestheticism and Morality," 30–31.

I am the hounded slave, I wince at the bite of dogs,
Hell and despair are upon me . . .
Agonies are one of my changes of garments,
I do not ask the wounded person how he feels,
 I myself become the wounded person,
My hurts turn livid upon me as I lean on a cane and observe.[34]

Democratic individuality is thus sustained by a poetic, "unreserved love" for, and identification with, all things in the world; in short, by a "new way of being in the world."[35] But it is crucial to understand that this poetic love is not characterized by a possessiveness or fusion of some sort. The gesture of identification is balanced by one of distinction or detachment. One of Whitman's greatest contributions, according to Kateb, is to have caught this sense of balance. It is marvelously expressed in the following lines, again from "Song of Myself":

Apart from the pulling and hauling stands what I am,
Stands amused, complacent, compassionating, idle, unitary,
Looks down, is erect, or bends an arm on an impalpable certain rest.
Looking with side-curved head curious what will come next,
Both in and out of the game and watching and wondering at it.[36]

This aesthetic of attachment/detachment is necessary to the ethos of democratic individuality because it keeps the bond of connectedness from becoming too sticky. It keeps me from investing myself too unreservedly in connections with those who are closest to me, those who are of my group, nation, or culture. My attention must always be ready to move on, outward, over the present horizon. This kind of promiscuous, poetic receptivity instantiates an "impersonal" moment of identity through which I am drawn beyond my "social enclosures," as well as out of any tendency to mere absorption in the life of my own personality.[37]

This ideal of receptivity, whereby one is always moving beyond the familiar, the conventional, and the comfortable, makes for a life full of risks, even a heroic one. Kateb does not think that one can live at such heights all the time, but one can persistently cultivate "moods, moments and episodes" of such receptivity, and these in turn can "gradually build up the overt connectedness" that best sustains a democratic culture.[38]

[34] *IO,* 153. The lines from "Song of Myself" are quoted on 263.

[35] *IO,* 153, 165.

[36] Quoted in *IO,* 261.

[37] *IO,* 163–65; "Democratic Individuality," 197. In *HA,* Kateb affirms some of these attitudes under the rubric of "moderate alienation," 178–79.

[38] *IO,* 32, 256, 258.

2.1.B. Resisting the Momentum of Reconciliation

Despite his intense admiration for the Emersonian tradition, Kateb is painfully aware that an idea of democratic individuality drawn exclusively from that source remains indebted to the idea of a divine creator of the world. However unorthodox the Emersonians were in relation to the Christianity of their day, the fact remains that theirs is a world that is theistically underwritten. The strength of their unorthodoxy is in how they resist the more normal religious tendency toward moral rigorism, where one is continually incited to divide the world into good and evil agents. As Whitman puts it, we must engage the other "not as the judge judges but as the sun falling around a helpless thing."[39] The Emersonians' will to see beauty in all particulars and to express a promiscuous love of the world did indeed restrain their propensity to either a moral rigorism or a narrow aestheticism: they were generally reluctant to judge harshly, condemn precipitously, or see ugliness easily. But such a bearing cohered only because the bad, the criminal, and the ugly are all ultimately reconciled within a beneficent, transcendent design.[40]

For us today, the comfort of meaning provided by such a design is too naive, too immediately innocent; it fails, Kateb suggests, to confront squarely enough the enormous cruelties and injustices that have been deliberately perpetrated, especially in the twentieth century. The certainty of divine reconciliation underlying the Emersonians' orientation to the beauty of all things endorses an absolving and affirming of the world that forgives such horrors too quickly. In effect, these nineteenth-century men are still subtly "craving" that the world *be for us; be intended for* reconciliation.[41]

How can one fold the momentum of this craving back upon itself in a way that nevertheless continues to draw sustenance from the Emersonian insights? For this purpose, Kateb articulates another moral source in addition to the sheer spectacle of particularity. He suggests that we try to cultivate an attachment to "existence as such" that is different from an attachment to particulars premised upon redemption.[42] Here he looks to Nietzsche and Heidegger for at least some hints as to how to proceed.[43]

For Nietzsche, of course, the world as a whole is not morally designed; and it is, as a consequence, simply beyond moral judgment, unencompassable in its indefiniteness. For Kateb, this means we do best to "remain

[39] Quoted in *IO,* 168. Of course, as Kateb notes, this sentiment has Christlike qualities.

[40] *IO,* 30, 245; *ESR,* 64–65, 92.

[41] *ESR,* 92–93; *IO,* 34–35, 169.

[42] *IO,* 128–30.

[43] Kateb offers what he calls a "ruthless and selective" reading of certain aspects of these philosophers' thoughts (*IO,* 145).

in incommensurability, disposed neither to forgive [evil] nor to think forgiveness is necessary."[44] In such an attitude, we allow ourselves neither to be enlisted easily in a moralized destructiveness aimed at ridding the world of evil, nor to absolve simply those who do evil.

Heidegger, in turn, helps us discern the kind of aesthetic-affective bearing that might emerge with and help sustain such an attitude toward existence. That attitude can become attachment insofar as we open ourselves to a "radicalized wonder": not the "immemorial wonder" at the world's supposed harmony or design, but rather a wonder that there is—as Heidegger puts it—*something* rather than *nothing;* that there *just is* existence as such. It is the sublimity of this radicalized wonder that can help bind us to the world.[45]

A strong sense of the inessentiality of all things engenders for Heidegger that attentive attitude he calls *Gelassenheit,* a letting be of things in the world, a relaxing of the urge to transform them, to make them conform to human purposes.[46] Although the idea of *Gelassenheit* resonates well with Kateb's own sense of the need to chasten human cravings, it is, by itself, too passive an attachment to capture fully the posture Kateb wants to affirm. Heidegger failed to see that today the threat of nuclear extermination of life shifts the terms of attachment to existence in a fundamental way: the inessentiality of things, their precariousness, now has a novel relation to human choice. Inaction carries its own danger. Attachment to existence thus must finally be a "preserving, protective attachment" that actively resists destructiveness. Kateb remains, however, relatively vague about what this call to "act with others" actually involves and when one should engage in it. Mainly the obligation seems to involve being suspicious of political authority and resistant to state activism: "Remote as the connection may seem, the encouragement of state activism, or the failure to resist it, contributes to nuclear statism and thus to the disposition to accept and inflict massive ruin and, with that, the unwanted and denied possibility of extinction."[47]

There is, for Kateb, no rational, ontological, emotional, or any other kind of necessity to this ethical commitment. At most, the thinking through of the inessentiality of existence as such and the cultivation of radicalized wonder can draw us toward making it. And even this pull must in turn draw sustenance from the Whitmanian attachment to the beauty of particulars. One must already "be schooled in beauty to sustain wonder that there is earthly existence rather than none."[48]

[44] *IO,* 143.
[45] *IO,* 147; *HA,* 165–66, 172.
[46] *IO,* 147–49.
[47] *IO,* 123, 147, 150, 164.
[48] *IO,* 149.

In effect, then, Kateb replaces the single moral source of God with two sources, neither of which, alone, is final or straightforwardly moral. Together, these *amoral* sources—the indefiniteness and inessentiality of existence as such and the spectacle of particulars—"correct and enhance" one another, but this mutual sustenance is cultivated, not designed.[49]

The resulting ontological array is thus indeed a folded one; the urge or craving for coherence, certainty, and wholeness is diffused and rendered more visible. Such a construction carries a number of the key hallmarks of a weak ontology: a sense of historical embeddedness, a strong appreciation of the aesthetic-affective dimension, and an emphatic thematization of natality. But there are, as well, some weaknesses that become apparent from the perspective of weak ontology as a whole. First, the engagements with language and finitude are minimal. I will come back to these issues in section 2.2. For the moment, I want to take up a problem that emerges around the issue of an ontological fold.

Despite my admiration for the subtle way in which Kateb's constellation effects a fold, this very gesture moves in quiet tandem with an underlying, intense certainty that works at cross-purposes with that fold. Speaking of his notion of amoral sources, Kateb states flatly that "belief in God is death to such an idea." The necessary poisonousness of theism is asserted with uncharacteristic certainty. This surety of meaning allows a fundamentalist thread to be wound into the narrative of modern democracy, as well as Kateb's own understanding of his place in it. With the tone of a retrospective prophet, he announces darkly that "the hidden source of democracy may always have been the death of God."[50] The momentum of this suggestion throughout Kateb's work largely cancels the apparent qualification carried by the tentative "may" in his explicit expression. Accordingly, Kateb knows his calling in history: he must fully secularize the Emersonians. As the quotation I cited at the beginning of the chapter (section 2.1.A) attests, Kateb sees himself as simply nudging them further along the world-historical, secular slope, upon which they still stick a bit, because they were, after all, still fooling themselves.[51]

The more one ponders this streak of atheistic fundamentalism, the more its assumption of certainty astonishes. In his constructive ontological gestures, Kateb is marvelous at making almost tactilely apparent the unrelenting strain of his efforts to constitute basic meanings. The craving

[49] *IO,* 153.

[50] *IO,* 8, 150, 171.

[51] The imperative and stakes of this struggle with religiosity are starkly apparent throughout *ESR* especially. Kateb concludes that when Emerson expresses religious thoughts, he "appears to be mesmerizing himself" (92).

for unity of meaning is thus not allowed to camouflage its tracks, but is continually folded back on itself. Basic meanings never slide effortlessly into mutual alignment; rather one feels their weight and friction continually. For example, there is no doubt that Kateb, like Whitman, wants us to feel the uplift of delight as we cultivate a sense of the beauty of particulars; but he knows also, like Thoreau, that cultivation is hard and unrelenting work.[52]

All of these admirable insights merely highlight the peculiarity of Kateb's devastating certainty in regard to theism. Of course, he might retort here that he must, when pushed, respond to religion's certainty with his own defensive certainty. In relation to many forms of theism, he is probably correct. But as the next chapter will show, theism in political thought perhaps does not have to follow such a script of certainty and intolerance. If this is so, then Kateb's weak ontology may be guilty of its own residual craving to shore up its fundamental meanings in illicit ways.

2.2. From an Emersonian Ontology to Ethics and Politics

For a weak ontology it is misleading to imply that there is a sharp categorical distinction between the ontological concepts, on the one hand, and ethical-political insight, on the other. Kateb's sketch of an Emersonian ontology is inextricably linked to questions of modernity and democracy. Thus, my elucidation of the ontology so far has already unavoidably begun to display a number of these entanglements. In this section, I begin to look more carefully at the way in which Kateb thinks his ontological articulations help prefigure a specific bent in ethics and politics. As I indicated in chapter 1, the claim that a weak ontology prefigures ethical-political life refers to how the former provides cognitive focusing and an affective attachment to the latter. Kateb, it seems to me, thinks in precisely such terms. There is never any question of the ontology's necessarily *entailing* any specific moral principle or public policy.[53] We, at most, gather various "considerations" that together provide a positive construal of the point of certain values and institutions; and, by contrast, throw other values and institutions under a shadow of suspicion, creating thereby a burden of proof against them.[54]

The ontological accounts of separateness and connectedness prefigure, respectively, the value of individual rights and constitutional democracy, and the significance of equal recognition. The first prefiguration

[52] Cf. *ESR,* 8–9. Democratic aestheticism "strains to submit the unbeautiful and the unsublime to aesthetic attitudes and feelings" ("Aestheticism and Morality," 33).

[53] *IO,* 5, 153, 259, 264; *ESR,* 201.

[54] Cf. *IO,* 93, 141–42.

is, I think, quite persuasive. It provides an admirable way of thinking about the enduring value of individualism. The second prefiguration, intended of course to be intimately related, is more problematic. The difficulties emerge in several places. First, there is a problem with the specific way the figure of "democratic connectedness" actually construes the idea of equal recognition (section 2.2.A). Second, there is some lack of coherence in the way Kateb understands the relationship between his ontology and the context of cultural meanings, *within which* that ontology is embedded but also *against which* it should provide resources for moral-political critique (section 2.2.B).

2.2.A. Connectedness and Separateness

Given the general intentions of my engagement with Kateb's rethinking of liberalism, I have been emphasizing the figuration of connectedness in his account of the "way of being" that is democratic individuality. This emphasis is not, I think, misplaced; we are told after all that the "highest purpose" of democratic individuality "is to establish a new sort of connectedness."[55] Although I have noted that this connectedness is related as well to a kind of separateness or detachment, the precise character of that relation must be elucidated a bit more. After this is done, one can see more clearly the distinctive prefiguration Kateb provides for the affirmation of individual rights and representative democracy. And once that sketch is in place, one can then better assess the overall ethical and political implications of the Emersonian notion of connectedness.

A dimension of detachment is absolutely crucial to Kateb's self, just as it is to other ideas of individualism. But the role of detachment in the former differs radically, in that self-centeredness is envisioned as a necessary gathering point for the cognitive, affective, and volitional powers of that receptiveness to the world that Whitman so marvelously displays. Hence, that tough, individual "self-reliance," as Emerson calls it, does not methodically trace its own enclosed orbit, but rather continually prepares new openings. As Kateb puts it: "One stays within oneself in order to enter imaginatively into all the commitments social life displays."[56] One remains self-reliant, then, precisely in order to become available to others; in order to vivify the connectedness of souls.

The character of *this* kind of connectedness is deadened, however, when the self is imagined as essentially encumbered by any sort of collective identity. An ontology conceived around *that* kind of connectedness

[55] "Democratic Individuality," 192.

[56] *ESR,* xxviii, 5; *IO,* 98–99.

only valorizes and legitimizes the "craving" for meaning discussed earlier. In so doing, it lends force to one of the deepest sources of human evil.[57]

Given the centrality of self-concern and self-reliance, it is hardly surprising to find Kateb asserting the absolute significance of protecting individual rights, since the effects of craving collective identity are most dangerous when manifested through the force of law. Now clearly part of Kateb's affirmation of rights is related to the familiar liberal claim that they simply create spaces for individuals. But if one thinks in these terms alone, that is, in terms of spaces created by a morally neutral, constitutional framework, then one substantially misses the distinctiveness of the prefigurative support the Emersonian ontology gives to such practices and institutions. Kateb wants us to think of them not as neutral but as "engender[ing] a distinctive culture," more specifically one in which the ethos of democratic individuality can flourish. Whatever else they do, the ongoing activities of claiming rights and electing leaders within a constitutional framework have the subtle effect of generating "an independence of spirit" in individuals, a continual pressure toward the democratization of social spheres outside politics, and a "sense of moral indeterminacy" born of the experience of respectful partisanship in regard to what is the "right" answer on any question animating the public. Additionally, the rhythm of representative democracy with its sporadic, rather than continual, involvement of individuals fosters a kind of "engaged detachment" or "distant citizenship." Such orientations are valuable because they support the "negative" political action necessary whenever governments threaten rights, but provide little susceptibility for enlistment in grand political projects aimed at "making over" social relations.[58] Through such socialization effects, constitutional democracy not only guards but indirectly helps further engender the ethos of democratic individuality.

But for such an ethos to really flower, these aggregate effects must be further cultivated by work on the self. It is only through the conscious micropractices of democratic aestheticism that the "highest purpose" of this distinctive individuality will be achieved; only with those practices do we bring to life that connectedness which is "the culmination of democratic justice."[59]

I want to turn now more directly to this question of the character of the democratic justice that is supposed to be nourished by Kateb's ontology. The core micropractice through which one does justice to the other is an act of identification. The other is disclosed to me by the projection of myself onto her or him in an identifying gesture. This moment is

[57] *IO,* 209.

[58] *IO,* 20, 38–45.

[59] "Democratic Individuality," 192, 197.

starkly captured in one of the passages from "Song of Myself" quoted earlier: "I do not ask the wounded person how he feels, / I myself become the wounded person." There is no doubt that this way of conceiving the ontological disclosure of the other to self may nourish a rich poetic sensibility. Moreover, it may also sustain certain highly admirable moral acts. One thinks here of Whitman's extraordinary and sustained generosity in caring for soldiers wounded in the Civil War.[60] Despite these aesthetic and moral attractions, there is a danger here, *at least when it is the value of justice that is being prefigured.* Such an oceanic self who washes over others may too easily, if unintentionally, become an agent of inundation.[61] There is a potential deafness here to the voice of the other. In a curious sense that voice becomes almost entirely dispensable. Whitman, in "Song of Myself," says as much: "I act as the tongue of you."[62] My concern here has to do with whether such an ontological figuration of self and other actually draws us toward "the best interpretation of the democratic idea that equals must be treated equally," or whether *the utterance of the other* has to find a more central place in the account.[63]

The reason for Kateb's relative deafness to this issue seems clear. As I have shown, what ultimately underlies his faith in the success of identity projections is the notion of the sameness of secular souls. They are literally alike; each contains "the same desires, inclinations and passions as well as aptitudes and talents." Given this sameness, the actual utterance of the other becomes decidedly secondary, because in a deep sense I already know—at least potentially—what is to be said. Thus, I can, without harm, comprehend the diversity of otherness as "an enactment, on a large scale, of private events" in the life of my own self.[64] But do I really do democratic justice to the diverse claims of others when I imagine that every line they might utter can be scripted in advance by me in my own private theater?[65]

[60] See Philip Callow's biography, *Walt Whitman: From Noon to Starry Night* (London: Allison and Busby, 1992); cf. *IO,* 2.

[61] Cf. Rosenblum, "Strange Attractors," 581–82.

[62] Whitman, "Song of Myself," in *Leaves of Grass,* intro. G. W. Allen (New York: New American Library, 1980), 93. The potentially inundating quality of the infinite self may be related to Whitman's affirmation of "adhesive love," as well as his rampant nationalism. Cf. Rosenblum, "Strange Attractors," 579–80. Kateb explicitly distances his reading of Whitman's ontology and its ethical political implications from such affirmations, but he does not attempt to explain why Whitman might have been drawn to them.

[63] "Walt Whitman and the Culture of Democracy," *Political Theory* 18, no. 4 (1990): 557. A modified version of this article forms the last chapter of *IO.*

[64] *IO,* 245; *ESR,* 15.

[65] In the introduction to *IO,* Kateb indicates that the presumption of identity is not always appropriate (34). Sometimes it is better to start, as Thoreau often did, with the presumption of nonaffinity. But Kateb does not follow up these brief remarks in any sustained fashion.

Kateb would likely defend himself against such charges of deafness and inundation of the other by recalling that the identitarian gesture of democratic aestheticism, because of its detachment and mobility, can never lend itself to grand political schemes in which others are shoved about in a paternalistic manner. One should grant Kateb this point. But paternalism is hardly the only danger here. For his "distant" citizens the greater trouble lies perhaps more with a failure really to grasp the nature of claims put forward by, say, movements seeking some sort of political recognition. Certainly the virtues of democratic aestheticism involve a generosity of attention to others. But the model of attention-giving is overly dependent on a visual metaphor; in effect, I can "act as the tongue of you" because I have *seen* you fully. For the Emersonians, "to *see right* is . . . the highest manifestation of justice" (my emphasis).[66]

I would suggest that the use of such a visual metaphor to represent the process of understanding is likely to be particularly susceptible to engaging the world in subtly depoliticizing ways. The point here is not that there is lack of intention to attend to others and see them as admirable, but rather that I may often fail to comprehend how my own interpretive frameworks unobtrusively structure the terms according to which I will extend my attention or the sentiment of admiration. For example, the Emersonian self could admire the quirky and impertinent behavior of "street people" living on the sidewalks of Manhattan; and it could see a dignity there that continually pokes through their apparent craziness. Moreover, this self might, as a result of its receptive sensibility, argue that the police and public should tolerate and not harass these unfortunate individuals. Such "seeing" could, I think, both satisfy the demands of democratic aestheticism and yet remain insufficiently political in its comprehension of the phenomenon of street people in American cities today.

Kateb is not unaware of such dangers, nor of how philosophically unfashionable his insistence on identity is. But he thinks the dangers are overblown, particularly when measured against the effects that result from starting with the opposite assumption of the radical *difference* of the other human. It is "better to err on the side of presumptuousness" by assuming identity than on the side of "bafflement" by assuming radical difference, for the latter will likely in the end yield only "fear and disgust" in relation to the other.[67]

If this were the choice to be faced, perhaps Kateb would be right. But he has tendentiously constituted the choice as bipolar. The options, however, are more numerous. Starting from Kateb's perspective of iden-

[66] *ESR*, 50.
[67] *IO*, 265.

tity, one could think about ways of folding that assumption back upon itself, of continually, if not fully, detaching it from its force (or craving?), and thereby perhaps lessening its propensity for fostering presumptuousness and unpolitical perception. The ultimate goal here would be a rendering of connectedness that is more congruent with a specifically *democratic* justice. How might the beginnings of such a revision be cast ontologically? Consider here two existential universals, language and human finitude. In chapter 1, I suggested that they will be centrally figured in a felicitous weak ontology; and yet they are relatively neglected in the ontology of democratic individuality.[68]

Turning to language, I first want to make some general remarks about Kateb's curious neglect of it and then suggest something more specific about a place for the utterance of the other. In the world of democratic individuality, one simply "sees" or comprehends things and people, and then perhaps expresses that comprehension in language. It would be a bit petty to criticize Emerson or Whitman for such an account of human being, given the character of nineteenth-century philosophy. But it is somewhat peculiar, after the so-called linguistic turn in the twentieth century (especially as represented by Wittgenstein and Heidegger) to find Kateb adhering to this kind of picture. Our entanglement with language is simply too constitutive to permit a view that backgrounds it so starkly in the activity of comprehending the other. Kateb is certainly aware of this broadly shared judgment about the significance of language and its complexity in accounts of ourselves. Why then does he ignore it? Ultimately, I think it comes down to his fear that if we talk too much about our being constituted by language, embedded in common meanings and so on, we will have simply given away too many hostages to proponents of some variant of group identity. Better to background language and highlight instead the figuration of natality displayed in the spectacle of the particular and the protean force of self-reliance, imagined against the secure background of the identity of secular souls.

But the more one ponders this curious background that is posited beyond the work of interpretation, the more one realizes that its plausibility tacitly (and ironically) depends on retaining just what Kateb strains to cleanse from the Emersonians: God. What could really securely guar-

[68] It should be noted briefly that what is lacking in the prefiguration of democratic justice is not made good by the notion discussed earlier of an attachment to existence as such. This sense of connectedness to the world, where one's fascination with, and wonder at, a world that has no purpose, is seen by Kateb as providing crucial motivation in support of acting to preserve that world. Such a stance is of no mean significance in a world with nuclear weapons, but this ethical purpose is not immediately helpful in relation to the question of an insightful way of construing the stickiness internal to a specifically democratic mode of relating self to other.

antee the sameness of souls? Could it be anything other than a divine creator postulated as their source? Once we cut the model of sameness loose from its religious moorings, however, then the emphasis upon the certainty of identity seems oddly forced. We just cannot plausibly project a fundamental identity of self and other, when they are now seen not as vessels afloat on an ocean of divine expression, but rather as natural creatures constituted by human expression.

Paradoxically, the portrait of a connectedness beyond language gives us a bond that is both too totalized and too escapable to serve the purpose of prefiguring democratic justice. There is indeed an admirable decentering of my personality that follows from the radicality of the insight that "every atom belonging to me as good belongs to you." But the feeling of dislocation thus evoked is at the very same time deeply disabled within Kateb's linguistically frictionless world. This is because the whole scene can be adequately represented as a play of characters within the private theater of my self's imagination. I am actor in, *and* director of, this performance; but since the characters only speak the lines I put in their mouths, the latter role remains invisible to me.

To repeat, the point of my critique is not to contend that the assumption of identity must be renounced altogether; it is rather to suggest that there are good reasons for both making it a more tentative starting point and allowing for more friction as this assumption engages the world. As a tentative starting point, identity or some kind of commensurability is quite plausible. As will be shown in the next chapter, Taylor marshals rather good arguments on this score (moreover, they do not rely upon his theism for their validity). And the friction that is lacking might be generated through the figuration of a distinctive ontological moment constituted by my confrontation with the utterance of the other. The utterance of the other human is a disclosure that calls me up short in a way no other natural object does, and in a way nothing I simply "see" does.

Jürgen Habermas is the philosopher most associated with the idea that the utterance of the other places an obligation upon me. I think there is a crucial notion in play here in his work, but it is typically overshadowed by the excessively precise normative character of the obligations he says we incur and by the underlying claim that an orientation to consensus is built into the telos of language.[69] Critics have, unsurprisingly, focused

[69] Habermas, *Knowledge and Human Interests,* trans. J. Shapiro (Boston: Beacon Press, 1971) 314. Cf. also *The Theory of Communicative Action,* trans. T. McCarthy, 2 vols. (Boston: Beacon Press, 1984), 1:287–88. This idea was reasserted in *The Philosophical Discourse of Modernity,* trans. F. Lawrence (Cambridge: MIT Press, 1987), 311.

their attention on such emphases. But one can refuse to follow Habermas in these more questionable claims and still prize the insight about the unpredictability and potential disruptiveness of the utterance in everyday life. Habermas wants us to attend to "a moment of *unconditionality*" in the utterance whereby the other comes to linguistic presence for me.[70] When we focus on *this* presencing, this natality or disclosure of particularity, we bear witness to the possibility of a no-saying to the identity I have projected onto the other, even when I am convinced that it is an appropriate figure of beauty.

This better accounting of language could be further enhanced if it were, in turn, brought into engagement with a more vivid rendering of mortality. As with language, Kateb tends to nudge finitude into the ontological background. And his justification for the latter move parallels the one for the former. As the editors of Kateb's Festschrift put it, he is leery of "finitude-fixated" philosophies, because they tend to render human being too needful, and thus too open to the warm comfort of reconciliation or redemption, whether its site be social, political, or religious.[71] This, for Kateb, poisons the idea of the infinite, "inner ocean" of each individual. But again, just as with the question of language, so with this question of finitude: Kateb simply considers too few options.

What if one were to cultivate a sense of finitude around the moment of individual linguistic disclosure, the moment in which I accept the immanent possibility that the reach of my interpretation will be brought up short? The particularity of this disclosure is not one suited to democratic aestheticism, at least in the sense of trying to see it as beautiful. Rather this might be taken as an experience around which to cultivate attitudes and feelings of sublimity; not a "sublime of quantity" such as Kateb finds appropriate to the wonder of existence as such in its overwhelming inessentiality and indefiniteness, but rather a quieter sublime associated with an everyday experience that speaks of my limits.[72] Such a thematization of finitude might arguably provide not a poisoning of individual infini-

[70] Habermas, *The Theory of Communicative Action,* 2:399; and *Philosophical Discourse of Modernity,* 322–23. Cf. Thomas McCarthy, *Ideals and Illusions: On Reconstruction and Deconstruction in Contemporary Political Theory* (Cambridge: MIT Press, 1991), 32–33.

[71] Austin Sarat and Dana Villa, "Liberalism, Modernism, and the Political Theory of George Kateb: An Introduction," in *Liberal Modernism and Democratic Individuality: George Kateb and the Practice of Politics,* ed. Sarat and Villa (Princeton, N.J.: Princeton University Press, 1995), 10–12.

[72] *IO,* 144. On this different way of thinking of the sublime, see my *Political Theory and Postmodernism* (Cambridge: Cambridge University Press, 1991); and the concluding chapter of *Edmund Burke: Politics, Aesthetics, and Modernity* (Thousand Oaks, Calif.: Sage Publications, 1994).

tude, but rather a chastening that folds it over upon itself and thereby brings it into a better congruence with our intuitions about democratic justice.

2.2.B. Democratic Recognition and Justice

I want to turn now finally to a closer consideration of how Kateb understands the relation of his ontology of individuality to the context of contemporary democracy. A weak ontology, as I have indicated, cannot claim a validity completely divorced from its context of cultural meanings. And yet the way in which it interprets those meanings should be capable of generating a critical edge that cuts, potentially at least, against the existing social status quo. This edge is formed by the specific prefigurative force the ontology provides. It seems to me that Kateb's understanding of democratic individuality fits this pattern well enough, for we are told that its core ideas help "to perfect the idealism already present, though imperfectly, in democratic life."[73] This perfectionism does not have a set telos; rather it merely aims at the persistent cultivation of a certain sensibility and a congruent orientation to ethical-political life. Each individual is to cultivate a willingness to transcend given social enclosures, identities, and conventions, and thereby open himself to the risk of what is beyond his present horizons. And when this task is taken up with the sensibility of democratic aestheticism, one will encounter others in a way that opens into equal recognition.

If Kateb thus has what is in general a plausible view of the relation of his ontology to its historical context, there is nevertheless a substantial problem in the specific way the critical force of the former actually cuts into the latter. In effect, Kateb presents a view of contemporary American democracy that is too politically self-satisfied. Now this judgment probably sounds as though it comes from a perspective external to Kateb's. And yet, interestingly, after he has fleshed out his position fully, he seems to be drawn to just such a judgment. But, and this is what I want to highlight, this concern on his part actually diverges from the very directions in which his explicit ontological articulations carry him. Thus, his dissatisfaction seems curiously external to his own project.

All this results finally, I think, from a certain deficit in ontological figuration. It is this deficit that, when combined with his broadly celebratory narrative of American democracy, makes for a picture of political life that is so contented that Kateb is moved finally to rebel a bit against his own conclusion. For my purposes, what is of particular interest is the question of which ontological figures might have been added to Kateb's

[73] *IO*, 27, 93, 154; cf. "Democratic Individuality," 190.

array in the first place, so that a more coherent rendering could have been given to those moral intuitions that end up surfacing unexpectedly in this rebellion.

Part of the problem has already been unearthed in the preceding section, where I suggested that democratic aestheticism produces a problematic prefiguration of equal recognition, in the sense that it is insensitive to certain sorts of claims that might be pressed in the name of democratic justice. This potential difficulty is compounded by the way Kateb portrays the existing context of political life in the United States. In describing the history and current reality of American democracy, Kateb continually emphasizes the extraordinary, operative power of its commitment to equal recognition: "The profound and immediate given—more purely in the American democracy than in any other—is equality." The force of that normative given suffuses this "most democratic culture in the world. Everywhere we look we see traces and often more than traces of the fundamental commitment to human equality." The dynamism of this commitment, first noticed by Tocqueville in the early nineteenth century, continues to assert itself forcefully in the United States at the beginning of the twenty-first century.[74]

Although Kateb's narrative of American democracy is thus a broadly celebratory one, it is not lacking altogether in critical resources. The ontology of democratic individuality certainly disposes one to avoid sustained political action to promote equal recognition, but it nevertheless remains sensitive to situations of egregious harm, where some collectivity (especially the state) threatens equal rights through specific acts. The critical edge that the ontology thus gives to the narrative of democracy is cast around "negative" or protective political action; one says no to clear violations of rights and is willing to act politically to block such assaults.[75] The actual behavior of the Emersonians themselves largely fits this model. One thinks of Thoreau's refusal to pay taxes that supported the United States' war against Mexico and of Emerson's protests against slavery, after his home state of Massachusetts agreed to abide by the Fugitive Slave Law of 1850, which required northern states to apprehend runaway slaves within their territory.[76]

Such negative political action is no doubt crucial to sustaining a notion of democratic connectedness and justice. But is it enough? Doesn't this critical edge in fact leave us with a view of contemporary political life in the United States that is more contented than it ought to be? Consider

[74] *IO,* 154–57.

[75] *IO,* 89; *ESR,* 34–35.

[76] For Emerson's position, see Robert D. Richardson, *Emerson: The Mind on Fire* (Berkeley and Los Angeles: University of California Press, 1995), 495–99.

the well-documented phenomenon of growing economic inequality since the 1970s. In the United States the distance between rich and poor appears to be widening faster than in other industrialized countries.[77] Kateb would, I think, be hard pressed to find many French or German visitors to this country today who have Tocquevillian reactions. My guess is that they would have more to say about our high poverty rate, homelessness problem, and inegalitarian health care system.

Our burgeoning inequality today is not easily described as the result of discrete state action. Thus, it would not seem to register as an event that would arouse Emersonian political dissent. But can such increasing inequality really be an object of relative indifference for any notion of democratic connectedness and justice?

Despite the many mistaken ideas Rousseau had about the ideal character of a democracy, he did put his finger on something crucial about economic inequality. Any sense of connectedness people have is impacted by the social-psychological distance between them. Growing economic inequality clearly thins out the commonality of our experience and thus our sense of connectedness. My point here is not to endorse the idea that democratic justice depends on achieving full economic equality for everyone. Rather it is only to question whether one can in good faith affirm democratic connectedness and justice as strongly as Kateb wants to and yet cast such suspicion upon any sustained political orientation toward addressing upwardly spiraling inequality. Kateb might object here that his democratic aestheticism teaches us precisely to ignore such distances between people as we work to vivify the identity of souls. But such a response only further intensifies a difficulty I noted earlier. Surely an ontology that urges us to take souls as identical, but that does so without divine guarantees, cannot be uninterested in the social forces that make the cultivation of such identification palpably harder.

But, as I pointed out a moment ago, Kateb rebels finally against the implications of his own position. In the introduction to the essays collected in *The Inner Ocean,* he affirms a "right . . . to be saved from material misery" as something necessary to human dignity. The duty to relieve misery, he writes, "is obligatory on society," and thus must become a "positive function" of government.[78] This affirmation, although admirable, sits rather uncomfortably with Kateb's general admonition against the common good of political projects. The resulting picture is of a state that

[77] See, for example, the data cited in Jeff Gates, *The Ownership Solution: Toward a Shared Capitalism for the Twenty-first Century* (Reading, Mass.: Addison Wesley, 1998), xix–xxvii, 2–9.

[78] *IO,* 2–3.

finds itself morally motivated to implement social programs on the basis of rights claims that somehow become pressing, even without active democratic movements behind them. My guess is that such a scenario of juridical-administrative state action is not a realistic one. If that is so, then the claims about alleviating material misery take on a slightly disingenuous quality, despite Kateb's intentions.

Kateb seems ultimately to sense this problem. In the conclusion of *Emerson and Self-Reliance,* he affirms an "interrupted self-reliance." Although he wants to root this orientation firmly in Emerson's ideas, it seems to be one in which the "interruptions"—political actions—take on a more independent significance. The experience of collective action, we are told, "can be . . . enlightening," in fact "a good in itself."[79]

These admissions strain against the boundaries of Kateb's project more than he is perhaps aware. His moral imagination is here expanding itself beyond anything he has articulated ontologically. For to speak affirmatively of the good of political action implies for it some more valued status than that of an external interruption for the otherwise contented democratic individual. Ultimately, Kateb has tacitly admitted that democratic aestheticism must find a way to admire *common* action in a noninstrumental sense. He can no longer imagine the world of democratic individuality to be one in which the only objects of beauty are individuals. Accordingly, what he owes us is a better ontological articulation of this new category. For someone so rooted in Emerson's sense of self-reliance, this will seem a deeply risky task. But if the imperative to take it on now appears to be internally unavoidable for an ideal of *democratic* connectedness, then it is a risk that must be faced. After all, risk taking of this moral-aesthetic sort is, as Kateb often reminds us, at the heart of Emersonian individuality.

[79] *ESR,* 200–201.

Chapter Three

THE "RICHER ONTOLOGY" OF CHARLES TAYLOR

NO THINKER TODAY has done more to press broad ontological questions than Charles Taylor. He has pursued this campaign for a number of years and been all too aware of how much his work has challenged "the current distribution of the onus of argument" in philosophy and social theory. The dominant, modern philosophical perspective has privileged a portrait of the self as essentially "disengaged" from its world. This self wants to gain epistemological purchase on, and practical control of, its world. It aims to master the terms of engagement. This is, of course, a kind of ontological perspective; but it has largely been assumed to be the only reasonable one. This has fostered "a kind of eclipse of ontological thinking" in contemporary moral and political theory.[1] Sometimes this has bordered on "motivated suppression" of ontological reflection, Taylor asserts, an orientation seen as justified "because the pluralist nature of modern society makes it easier to live that way."[2] Too much emphasis on ontological fundamentals will only rigidify lines of division between different ways of seeing the world and the human predicament.

If one of the theses of this book is correct, however, a growing number of thinkers have concluded that the simple avoidance of ontology is a bad strategy in the face of late modern concerns. The costs of a commitment—either explicit or implicit—to a "disengaged" view of the self now

The following abbreviations will be used for referring to Taylor's books.

- *HAL* — *Human Agency and Language.* In *Philosophical Papers,* vol. 1. Cambridge: Cambridge University Press, 1985.
- *PA* — *Philosophical Arguments.* Cambridge: Harvard University Press, 1995.
- *PAH* — *Philosophy and the Human Sciences.* In *Philosophical Papers,* vol. 2. Cambridge: Cambridge University Press, 1985.
- *PAP* — *Philosophy in the Age of Pluralism.* Edited by James Tully. Cambridge: Cambridge University Press, 1994.
- *POR* — *"The Politics of Recognition."* In *Multiculturalism: Examining the Politics of Recognition,* edited by Amy Gutmann. Expanded ed. Princeton, N.J.: Princeton University Press, 1994.
- *SS* — *Sources of the Self: The Making of Modern Identity.* Cambridge: Harvard University Press, 1989.
- *RS* — *Reconciling the Solitudes: Essays on Canadian Federalism and Nationalism.* Edited by Guy Laforest. Montreal: McGill-Queen's University Press, 1993.

[1] "Cross-Purposes," in *PA,* 185.

[2] *SS,* 10.

outweigh those encountered when we rethink the self as part of a "richer ontology."[3] But if the onus of philosophical argument has begun to fall a little less heavily on those pursuing paths of richer ontological reflection, it is still true that Taylor's thought draws upon itself a kind of suspicion that is not attracted by a thinker like Kateb. The latter is staunchly secular and thoroughly liberal. Taylor, on the other hand, is "a Christian and . . . a Hegelian," as Isaiah Berlin succinctly puts it. Accordingly, Taylor's critics assume that he is offering a return to what I have called strong ontology; that is, some foundationalist, determinate truth about the shape and direction of self and world. As this suspicion emerges, it energizes a couple of interpretive prejudices that allow Taylor to appear hopelessly weak from the start. The first is that Taylor's views are, well, philosophically outdated, and thus, however complex they might be, not worth much serious thought. The second would have us take Taylor seriously, but less for his insights than for the danger that emerges from his work. Thus Quentin Skinner warns us that Taylor has placed himself on a slippery, theistic-Hegelian slope, at the end of which lie intolerance and coercion.[4] Skinner's critique buttresses the default judgment of many liberals today that I mentioned earlier: too much talk of ontology is bad for a pluralistic society.

Are these criticisms fair? Is Taylor really just offering a reiteration—albeit a very clever one—of a traditional, theistic mode of strong ontology? Or is something more novel in play, something closer to weak ontology? I think the correct answers here are, respectively, no and yes. In order to make these claims plausible I will show in this chapter that Taylor's project lends itself quite well to analysis in terms of the aspects of weak ontology I have delineated.[5] It claims to tell us something deep or

[3] "Explanation and Practical Reason," in *PA,* 39. Taylor sometimes uses the term *philosophical anthropology* to describe his project, rather than *ontology.* Given the traditional connotations of the latter term, this seems appropriate. But Taylor is himself not entirely satisfied with the former term. I think that my notion of weak ontology would be largely appropriate for the kind and level of philosophical reflection he has in mind; cf. *SS,* 514–15. He speaks, for example, of the "ontology of human life: what kinds of things you invoke in talking about human beings in the different things we do: describing, deliberating, judging"; "Rorty in the Epistemological Tradition," in *Reading Rorty,* ed. Alan Malachowski (Oxford: Blackwell, 1990), 261.

[4] I have heard the first of these criticisms expressed at conferences, but not in print. For the second, see Quentin Skinner, "Who Are 'We'? Ambiguities of the Modern Self," in "Symposium on Charles Taylor's *Sources of the Self,*" *Inquiry* 34 no. 2 (1991): 133–53. The quotation is from Isaiah Berlin, introduction to *PAP,* 1.

[5] In an earlier essay, I spoke of Taylor as "a border runner between strong and weak ontology." I now think this judgment mistaken. Taylor is squarely within the terrain of weak ontology. See "Weak Ontology and Liberal Political Reflection," *Political Theory* 25 no. 4 (1997): 506.

essential about human being and world; and this portrait is one that emphasizes the self's stickiness or embeddedness, its partial constitution by language and the world. And yet, in this reaching for depth, Taylor's project nevertheless brings into play resources for attuning itself to its own limits (section 3.1). In addition, this ontology accords a crucial place to decidedly modern insights about aesthetic-expressive experience, even as it locates itself in a theistic view of the world. The resulting perspective ends up being pretty remote from the one toward which the aforementioned critics direct their fire (section 3.2). If my arguments in sections 3.1 and 3.2 are valid, then Taylor's ontological formulations are related to his explicit moral-political claims in a fashion more typical of weak ontology than of strong ontology; in short, the latter are prefigured, not simply determined, by the former (section 3.3).

3.1. Engaged Agency

The propensity of modern philosophy and social theory to begin with a disengaged self oriented toward scrutinizing its possible terms of world-engagement betrays, according to Taylor, a willful neglect of ways in which the self is always already engaged, embedded, or situated. Human agency is partially, but deeply, constituted by this engagement with the world. A richer ontology is, accordingly, one that gives us a better sense of the facets of this relationship. Only on the basis of such an elucidation of the conditions of possibility of selfhood or agency can one adequately engage questions of epistemology, ethics, and politics.[6]

Methodologically, then, Taylor deploys an argument of conceptual necessity, in order to generate a set of existential universals. This strategy for getting at depth is, of course, a rather bold one in today's philosophical climate. Its apparently apodictic quality evokes strong skepticism. Claims about agency *in general,* rather than agency in historical-cultural context, are notoriously difficult to sustain, at least if they go beyond certain uncontroversial minima.

Given this bind, it becomes more understandable why a theorist like Kateb largely steers around the issue of universality in relation to his ontological constellation—self, soul, personality, other, and existence as such. It is difficult not to think that a universality claim is attached to at least some of these concepts. But Kateb argues for the coherence of his constellation only in the context of the meaning of "living in a rights based democracy."[7] If Kateb has chosen to leave his universality claim largely indeterminate, Taylor has opted to push his very hard. He con-

[6] Preface to *PA*, vii ff.

[7] *IO,* 258; cf. 153–66.

tends that such a project can be fleshed out in a way that does not run roughshod over historical or cultural variation. Clearly this is an ambitious task.

In this section I begin to examine this project, how it construes depth and engagement ontologically and how it nevertheless admits its own contestable status. This requires, first, an analysis of what Taylor sees as the necessary features of any ontology, features implied by the very concept of agency (section 3.1.A). Second, I will elucidate his fascinating attempt in *Sources of the Self* to show that modern, Western questions about identity are best explored in terms of different sets of ontological constellations that are more historically porous than the array of concepts he associates with the identity of agency as such (section 3.1.B).

3.1.A. The Background of Agency

Taylor's ontological reflections are best understood when one distinguishes three levels. The first includes those concepts necessary to map the "space of questions" in which human being is embedded. This level constitutes a template of "inescapable questions," as it were, onto which any specific ontological constellation must be capable of being inscribed. A second level of inquiry concerns which constellations provide insightful and perspicuous interpretations of the diverse character of modern, Western identity; in short, which "fit" cogently with a historically constituted "us." Finally, a third level broaches the issue of which of the interpretively reasonable constellations is actually the best for a late modern West. Already beginning to separate himself from strong ontology, Taylor says that the second two levels of reflection involve "contestable answers to inescapable questions." It is to the level of supposedly invariable questions that I want to turn first.[8]

An agent is always already reacting to and evaluating situations that confront it, and doing so against an implicit set of background commitments. The character of this background or lifeworld cannot be illuminated by considering it as a possible object to be comprehended in an attitude of full disengagement. Rather the background is partially constitutive of oneself. Gaining clarity here requires trying to reconstruct, from within the agent's perspective, how this background structures one's reactions and evaluations. Taylor refers to this mode of analysis as "a phenomenological account of identity" or an internal account of "what it is to be an agent."[9]

[8] *SS,* 41, 529.
[9] *SS,* ix, 29, 32.

Situations strike us. Some do so in ways that are relatively simple conceptually, such as when a high-pitched sound causes pain or a wonderfully prepared dish elicits the comment "delicious." Others evoke more complex reactions such as indignation, shame, remorse, admiration, condemnation, and so on. Here our capacity for ethical discrimination in its broadest sense is entwined with feeling or sentiment. Too often in contemporary moral philosophy, Taylor contends, this entanglement is marginalized in the name of getting a clear, rational purchase on moral judgment. But this strategy merely betrays the typical effect of an attachment to the idea of disengaged agency: a desire to start serious thought from outside of engagement. From within the standpoint of engaged agency, however, the connection of discrimination and feeling is intrinsic. Indeed, "feeling is our mode of access to . . . what it is to be human."[10] When we react in this fashion, we are engaged in "strong evaluations"; that is, we find our feelings articulated by rich languages of contrastive characterization that allow us to classify the actions, persons, and motivations we encounter as better or worse, higher or lower, worthy or unworthy, right or wrong.[11] In making such "qualitative distinctions," we draw upon, explicitly or implicitly, some "ontological account" of self and world: a "background picture" that portrays us as a certain type of creature in a certain type of world; say, creatures of God standing before divine judgment, or rational agents standing alone in a disenchanted universe. These pictures of our moral and "spiritual nature and predicament" structure our moral intuitions such that we "see-feel" some action as meriting a corresponding reaction. (Taylor uses "spiritual" here to include a wide range of concerns, from what constitutes a fulfilling life to one's sense of what is beyond the human.) In the broadest terms, background pictures allow us "to make sense of our lives" morally and spiritually, to articulate them as meaningful.[12]

Although Taylor sometimes describes this orienting role in terms of a map, the analogy is of limited use. At night, we might quickly resolve our uncertainty about direction by shining a flashlight on a map. We get full illumination of the whole terrain. Background pictures, however, orient us only through incremental interpretation; we "articulate" them through language as we reflect upon our specific moral reactions. Full articulacy, like full control of our language, is an illusion.[13] Embeddedness is a condition of human being, not an optional or dispensable stance.

[10] "Self-Interpreting Animals," in *HAL*, 6; and *SS*, 8.

[11] "What Is Human Agency?" in *HAL*, 15–23; *SS*, 4.

[12] *SS*, 3–8, 18, 74. Taylor uses the term "see-feel" in "Self-Interpreting Animals," 70.

[13] "What Is Human Agency?" 35 ff.; "Self-Interpreting Animals," 62 ff.; and *SS*, 8, 18, 77–80.

There is, for Taylor, no coherent way to stand outside the orienting force of background pictures. Such embeddedness is constitutive of the very notion of having an identity. "Our identity is what allows us to define what is important to us and what is not." The idea of a person without a background framework altogether is the idea of a person outside our normal sphere of interlocution; in short, "pathological."[14]

Above I pointed out the central role that feeling or sentiment plays within Taylor's analysis. This emphasis extends as well to the quality of background pictures. So far I have explicated them as something like metainterpretations that define the space within which the specific interpretations evident in our moral reactions take form. This way of seeing Taylor's point is not incorrect, but it is one-sided. Our background picture defines what is of "incomparable" importance to us, our good. And since it does, how we stand within its space is not a matter we can regard with detached indifference. "One of the most basic aspirations of human beings," Taylor tells us, is "the need to be connected with . . . what they see as good, or of crucial importance, or of fundamental value." This means that in regard to the space offered by our background picture, we are "not . . . able to stop caring where we sit."[15]

This necessary, affective attachment to what we take—however implicitly—to be "incomparably" good also throws our capacity for articulation into a new light. It is now no longer a primarily cognitive activity of working back and forth between text (situation and reaction) and context (background picture) so as to better comprehend both. Articulation, seen in affective terms, "can bring us closer to the good as a moral source, can give it power" in our lives. This empowering capacity of articulation, this ability to inflate "the lungs of the spirit," is largely missed when morality is conceived narrowly as simply a set of obligatory norms of right.[16]

In this portrait of a constitutive, affective pull, Taylor offers us his account of the existential universal of attachment to existence. One can come to terms with this attachment in different ways and cultivate it in different directions, but the peculiar force of the experience of attachment is distinctive to human being, and something that ethical-political life should not try to ignore.

Stepping back now from the ontological sketch of agency that has emerged in the last couple pages, one can ask: what is the exact philosophical status Taylor claims for his arguments? Clearly, as I noted earlier, it has something of the sense of a transcendental claim: he has laid out conditions of the possibility of agency. And yet Taylor speaks only of

[14] *SS*, 27, 30–31.

[15] *SS*, 42, 44.

[16] *SS*, 92–94, 520.

" 'transcendental conditions,' " being careful to insert scare quotes.[17] In order to get at just what the commitment here amounts to, consider how Taylor confronts counterarguments. The most immediately evident challenges would come not from premodern or non-Western modes of thought, many of which might fit plausibly within Taylor's ontological template. Rather they come from modern, Western views such as utilitarianism. This school of thought, as Taylor is well aware, would not find the idea of incomparable goods and background pictures at all necessary to its way of imagining our moral life. Agents simply label things according to the amount of pleasure they would provide and then calculate what combination would maximize their overall happiness. Accordingly, morality becomes simply a matter of determining, across agents, what arrangement yields the greatest net happiness, and a background picture or framework is a fifth wheel. Taylor counters that, if we attend carefully to the utilitarian's account, we will see that he in fact "doesn't lack a framework" within which strong evaluation proceeds. In reality "he has a strong commitment to a certain ideal of rationality and benevolence. He admires people who live up to this ideal, condemns those who fail or who are too confused even to accept it, feels wrong when he himself falls below it." The utilitarian does indeed live "within a moral horizon" of the sort Taylor describes, only he cannot give any account of it *within his own moral theory*.[18]

In *Sources of the Self,* one of the central purposes is to reconstruct modern traditions like utilitarianism and show that they can give plausible accounts of themselves only if they invoke the language of background pictures, moral sources, and so on; in other words, if they accept the idea of an ontological space of inescapable questions. This does not, of course, mean that the central moral sources of such traditions must be substantively the same as for, say, a theistically based morality. Taylor's primary intention in the book is not to declare a specific, substantive ontological constellation the one true ground for modern identity, but rather to show that the *diversity* of modern identity is best understood as a bundle of answers to questions that are constitutive of agency as such.

In the answer Taylor provides to his utilitarian opponent, one can begin to see how he wants to distinguish, and yet not completely separate, the necessary space of agency from its fuller and variable historical manifestations. Sometimes, however, he does seem to speak as though he can fully insulate the former sphere from the latter and give it an unshakable defense. In this vein, he maintains that the picture of agency explicitly defended by utilitarians is that of a "monster," something simply beyond

[17] *SS,* 32.
[18] *SS,* 31.

the concepts that define us humans.[19] Taylor is nevertheless aware that he has no philosophical means of establishing an absolutely incontestable boundary for us/monsters. Accordingly, he admits that his appeal to conceptual necessity is in reality always open to contest. "The question is whether one could draw a convincing portrait of a subject" for whom the moral and affective logics implied in these core concepts were "quite foreign."[20]

Although Taylor is clearly doubtful about the prospects of such a counterportrait, it would be wrong to see his statement here as a rhetorical device designed to make his thought appear open when it is in reality effectively closed. As I have said, weak ontology must not only state its limits, it must actively fold back upon itself by embodying the force of that statement in its own logic. I will show how Taylor satisfies this requirement in a moment.

But consider first a likely objection to Taylor's project. If he has indeed admitted the possible porosity of his strong conceptualization of agency as such, what do his claims about its "necessity" really amount to? Why not simply jettison this template dimension of ontology and proceed, say, as Kateb does, sticking with the more modest task of reconstructing an ontological constellation corresponding to a relatively discrete historical formation like a contemporary "rights-based democracy"? In trying to answer this question, one can, I think, better comprehend how this deepest level of weak ontological reflection might be understood. Now clearly, its distinctiveness cannot derive from a claim about incontestable grounding. Rather the inescapability encountered at this level has to be seen as constituted by the limits of imagination. More specifically, Taylor would argue that he has tracked the limits of human imagination as he is capable of construing it. It is against the background of such a template that we can give the best accounts of more historically specific embodiments of that imagination. In elucidating these limits, Taylor is not claiming to have discovered a level of metaphysical bedrock. Rather, he is claiming that, from within the perspective of engaged, embodied agency, these limits operate for us in our moral-spiritual life analogously to the way "up" and "down," "here" and "there" operate for us in our physical life.[21]

And yet Taylor is well aware that we can reimagine things. He cannot close off the possibility of reimagining some aspect of his ontological template. The template's elucidation, however, constitutes for him a declaration of limits beyond which at present he cannot see.

[19] *SS,* 32.

[20] "What Is Human Agency?" 28.

[21] "The Validity of Transcendental Arguments," in *PA,* 30.

3.1.B. Western Ontological Constellations

One of the characteristics of a felicitous weak ontology is the persuasiveness with which an array of specific concepts of self, other, and world are located within a broad historical narrative (what I called a "grand narrative" in chapter 1). This dimension of moral-political affirmation—this "we" construction—carries with it, of course, substantial dangers. Given this prospect, some would argue that it is best simply to give up on such constructions. As with every other aspect of weak ontology, I want to suggest that such a strategy of nonaffirmation does not stand up well over time. A better alternative is to take on the affirmative burden of large narratives, but in such a way that one's story signals its own contestability.

In *Sources of the Self,* Taylor constructs what is certainly one of the grandest portraits of the modern West that has appeared in recent decades. Its account of something like the "deep meaning" of modern Western experience is almost painfully unfashionable. But if one puts this initial reaction aside and looks carefully, Taylor's narrative is not quite the easy target it first appears to be. At the heart of this narrative is an account of three ontological constellations that constitute what, for Taylor, are the dominant substantive answers that have emerged in the West to those inescapable questions mapped by the formal, ontological template I elucidated in the preceding section.

Taylor's ontological path to opening up the task of historical narrative gives him a distinctive angle from which to delineate both commonalities and divergences in the three substantive constellations he sketches. In the modern world there is a diffuse, broad agreement on some fundamental "life goods": individual freedom and universal justice; benevolence, especially the avoidance of suffering; and the affirmation of ordinary life, that is, the everyday sphere of family and work. This commonality rests, however, upon "profound rifts," fully apparent only when these life goods are placed within the different ontological constellations around which the dominant variations in modern identity cohere. The divergences relate to the highest, or "constitutive," goods—and thus the moral sources—that animate the imperatives we attach to the foregoing life goods. The first of these constellations is the original theistic one, within which God is the constitutive good. For an adherent of this constellation, the realization of life goods is construed as enhanced participation in the "divine affirmation of the human."[22]

The second constellation emerged with the Enlightenment. Taylor calls this the "naturalism of disengaged reason." The core ideas have

[22] *SS,* 495, 521.

taken many forms; some of them, such as utilitarianism, denying completely that they in fact imply any constitutive good. Taylor, as I indicated earlier, works extremely hard to demonstrate that such a mode of self-understanding is simply not coherent. Proponents of naturalism may fix upon a highest good that is not "external to man," such as love of humanity, but such a good has the constitutive and affective qualities that God manifests within the theistic constellation. In short, it functions as a moral source, "the contemplation of which commands" one's admiration and awe. The naturalists' "reductive ontology," however, prevents them from formulating and recognizing these sources. So the sources will thus typically do their work from behind the scenes, structuring the rhetoric and empowering the attack on the opponents of naturalism. Thus, the force provided by these sources is present, even when explicitly denied. We find it, for example, in Jeremy Bentham's "*cri de coeur* about the love of mankind," or in "the agnostic's austere commitment to progress," or in the Sisyphean struggle to relieve suffering in a disenchanted world, captured in a figure such as Camus's Dr. Rieux in *The Plague*.[23]

The third modern ontological constellation emerges out of romanticism and continues especially in certain strands of modern art and literature. It is a reaction against both orthodox theism, with its remote, commanding God, and naturalism, which increasingly reduced the natural world to a field of matter that we engage only instrumentally. Within the third constellation, the moral source is associated with individual creativity and expression, the power to make something meaningful manifest. This source may be conceived of as in a mutually constitutive relationship with some nonanthropocentric source, in the sense that our capacity for expression allows us to attune ourselves with the impulses of nature or come to an empowering construal of "the order in which we are set."[24] Within this constellation, the exploration of the beyond human takes a novel, modern form. The nonanthropocentric source is not understood as being like an object that we attempt to discover or to which we simply find access. Rather its being is constitutively tied to our powers of expression. Thus, in this way of understanding the exploration of nonanthropocentric sources, "Discovering. . . depends on, is interwoven with, inventing."[25]

But the creative self as source may also be conceived in a radically subjectivized sense, where sheer self-celebration in some form is the highest good. Taylor clearly finds this second variant of the ontological constellation formed in the wake of romanticism to be lacking. Such

[23] *SS*, 93–94, 324–25, 331–39, 496.
[24] *SS*, 496, 510.
[25] *SS*, 18.

"subjectivized expressivism," he argues, roots itself in an unwarranted certainty about the world that "means not only that it is closed to any theistic perspective, but that it can't even have a place for the kind of non-anthropocentric exploration of sources" that has characterized the first variant, for example in the works of Rainer Maria Rilke, Marcel Proust, Thomas Mann, T. S. Eliot, or Franz Kafka.[26]

Taylor's overall claim can now be stated as the assertion that the senses of modern identity are best understood as clustering around one or more of these three ontological constellations. In one sense, this is a broadly descriptive or interpretive claim; and the length of *Sources of the Self* is a result of Taylor's trying to make it persuasive across the expanse of Western ideas. But in other senses it is, of course, normative as well. Part of what he is suggesting is that the three constellations have established a terrain of reflection on our predicament; and that perspectives that try to wall off some part of this terrain as essentially unworthy of continued reflection are guilty of a kind of willful inattention to the terms of our predicament. It is just such a failure that Taylor finds in the radically subjectivized variant of the third constellation. It fails to keep itself uncertainly open to the terrain of contestation about human being and world that is itself part of what we moderns are.

Here one might suspect that Taylor is really just offering us a theistic, strong ontological wolf in weak ontological, sheep's clothing. But he is also critical of variants of theism that want to deny the central significance of subjective articulation of meaning and sensibility. We can't just willfully retreat behind this part of the modern terrain of consciousness to the certainty and objectivity of a God of commands.[27] In sum then, Taylor does indeed affirm a certain openness to ontological diversity.

This degree of affirmation of contestation would, however, hardly allay all suspicion. Taylor has certainly urged attentiveness to the full space of concerns occupied by the three ontological constellations. But one only has to reflect for a moment to think of various possible objections, in the light of which Taylor seems to be limiting the contestedness allowed. For example, is his ambitious interpretation of Western history correct in its conclusion that the ontological space of understanding is adequately covered by just his three constellations? Have significant voices and possibilities been shunted aside?

For Taylor, no interpretation is beyond contestation. The articulation of sources and the effort to understand the other's expressions are not secondary characteristics of our being. The work of understanding, of linguistically negotiating between the interpretations of self and other,

[26] *SS*, 490, 506–8, 510.
[27] *SS*, 512.

identity and difference, is a constitutive part of what we are. Borrowing here from Gadamer, Taylor expresses this thought succinctly: "*Verstehen* is a *Seinsmodus.*"[28] To imagine human being in this way means simultaneously that you also privilege the activity of dialogue or conversation, within which we bring our interpretations to bear. There simply is no foothold outside of conversation on which to put one's weight in order to assert that I "have got it simply right against all others."[29]

But such appeals to the final court of conversation are hardly likely to convince critics without further clarity on exactly what Taylor embraces in Hegel. This entanglement, when combined with Taylor's expressed hope for "reconciliation" of the voices in the conversation of humankind, gives at least some initial cause for concern.

In Taylor's discussions of conversation and reconciliation, it is in fact Gadamer rather than Hegel that is the leading figure. In this sense, there is no question of Taylor's believing that, say, intercultural conversations have some unifying, necessary telos.[30] There is, rather, only

> the idea of an omega point, as it were, when all times and cultures of humanity would have been able to exchange and come to an undistortive horizon for all of them. But even this would still be only de facto universal. If it turned out that one culture had been left out by mistake, the process would have to start again. The only possible ideal of objectivity in this domain is that of inclusiveness. The inclusive perspective is never attained de jure. You only get there de facto, when everybody is on board. And even then the perspective is in principle limited in relation to another possible understanding which might have arisen. But all this doesn't mean that there is no gain, no overcoming of ethnocentrism. On the contrary; it is overcome in inclusiveness.[31]

This Gadamerian ideal is, in effect, an ideal of possibility: the possibility of reconciliation between what seems at first to be irremediably in opposition or incommensurable. There are no guarantees, however, no necessity of progress. What this ideal primarily gives us is, in short, simply the motivation to "try and see" what progress can be made.[32]

Taylor does, of course, realize that the dominant conversations of Western modernity have often been carried on with a false, universalist self-understanding. But that, in itself, is not enough to warrant the view that, on principle, one should affirm a thorough relativism or incommensura-

[28] *SS,* 72, 233–34; "Heidegger, Language, and Ecology," in *PA,* 118.
[29] "Charles Taylor Replies," in *PAP,* 230.
[30] James Tully, preface to *PAP,* xiv–xv.
[31] "Comparison, History, Truth," in *PA,* 151.
[32] "Explanation and Practical Reason," 55.

bility of different forms of life. Taylor has, it seems to me, two grounds for refusing to accept such a perspective. First, he can point to historical instances where apparently irreconcilable orientations have reconceived themselves. "For a long time our ancestors couldn't conceive how to reconcile popular rule and public order. Now the most law-abiding societies are democratic."[33] A few historical examples like this are, however, a slim reed on which to rest the full weight of his ideal of the possibility of reconciliation. The real burden of argument must fall somewhere else; and that spot is his understanding of language and articulation. Taylor has not, to my knowledge, used this understanding to mount exactly the kind of argument I will present below, but I think it is suggested by the claims he has made.

Taylor is perfectly willing to admit that we may run up against irreconcilables or incommensurability in the mutual confrontation of forms of life, moral sources, and so on. The claim to know that such an outcome is inescapable *from the start,* however, betrays an implausible comprehension of the orientation of self to lifeworld. By *lifeworld,* I mean broadly the unthought of our thought, the implicit of our explicit, the unconscious background of our conscious foreground. *Background* in this sense has a broader reach than the notion explored earlier of "background picture"; the latter is one aspect of the former. Now the claim to know categorically that, say, one's form of life is irreconcilable with another would ultimately have to rest on a couple of other claims, both of which are implausible. First, it would have to rest on the assertion that one's form of life was in some sense fully available to oneself in all its implications and complexity. But since one's form of life is inextricably entangled with the language that interprets one's lifeworld in general, to claim that one has an exhaustive grasp of the former's boundaries and possibilities is thus also to claim that one has such a grasp of one's language and lifeworld. This is at root an astounding image of mastery. It is as if a person who is frustrated that she keeps missing things in the background of her visual field, because she is concentrating earnestly on something in the foreground, might simply decide to solve her problem once and for all by foregrounding everything.

For Taylor, linguistic articulation of that which is part of the inarticulate background that is one's lifeworld is always a partial achievement. We make something manifest, but it remains located against an enduring background, even if the latter is now different. The relationship of this linguistic manifestness to its background is represented by Taylor with the image of a web that is touched in one spot. A specific expression that makes something linguistically explicit cannot help but resonate

[33] "Charles Taylor Replies," 214.

through the background of that which is left implicit, the way the touching of a web resonates through the entire structure of filaments.[34]

The claim to possess a level of explicitness about one's form of life, moral source, and so on, sufficient to know its precise boundaries and thus to declare its irreconcilability with others from the start, also runs afoul of another characteristic of articulation. This is the fact that the activity of articulation, especially when it concerns our moral and spiritual life, has a potentially transformative or transvaluative effect:

> Much of our motivation—our desires, aspirations, evaluation—is not simply given. We give it formulation in words or images. Indeed by the fact that we are linguistic animals our desires and aspirations cannot but be articulated in one way or another. . . .
>
> . . . But this kind of formulation or reformulation does not leave its object unchanged. To give a certain articulation is to shape our sense of what we desire or what we hold important in a certain way.[35]

In expressing our thoughts and feelings, we are always engaged in an at least potentially transformative activity. Rephrasing this more precisely for present concerns, one would say that the very activity of articulating those things that are morally and spiritually crucial to one's form of life unavoidably puts one in a position of seeing/feeling them in new contexts and with new possibilities.[36] The clear implication of this is that any confident announcement of irreconcilability at the start must be seen as betraying a willful blindness to the possibility of new avenues of reconcilability opening up in the mutual articulation of conversation. Such an argument does not, of course, establish that reconciliation will emerge in any given case. It merely shows that the affirmation of irreconcilability, which often advertises itself as the ripe fruit of a renunciation of Western gestures of mastery, must in fact root itself in its own inconspicuous gesture of mastery.

Taylor does not explicitly identify this ethical failing of the rigid proponent of irreconcilability, but it is related to the way he describes how agents can be said to be "responsible for our evaluations." In our moral evaluations, we "strive to be faithful" to our "deepest unstructured sense" of what is of decisive importance; say, that "a certain mode of life [is] higher than others" or that "belonging to this community is essential to my identity."[37] But, as we saw above, this striving to keep one's bearing in moral space cannot be done honestly by simply holding tight to the

[34] "Language and Human Nature," in *HAL,* 231.

[35] "What Is Human Agency?" 36.

[36] "Heidegger, Language and Ecology," 107–9.

[37] "What Is Human Agency?" 35, 38, 40–41.

highest object of one aspirations. Honest striving, and hence acceptance of responsibility for one's evaluations, is realized only in a stance of careful attentiveness to possible shifts in the meaning such objects carry for us.

If this is indeed the philosophical sense of Taylor's orientation to conversation and reconciliation, then it would seem to have very little in it of the Hegel that liberals have rightly found disturbing. And yet Hegel remains an important philosopher for Taylor. Especially relevant in this context is Taylor's affirmation of the idea of human "potentialities" that can be realized in history. But even this notion is hedged with significant qualifications: there is no unitary set of potentialities, no unitary direction of unfolding, and no unfolding of potentialities that is pure gain; rather there is always gain and loss. Finally, the realization of a given potential, which allows one to speak of some gain and progress, is a story told for a civilizational "locality," in the sense that for modern Western identity, "The Greeks and we are in one 'locality.' "[38]

Although Taylor would want to defend a number of gains of this sort, such as a universalistic notion of rights, in the present context one gain is particularly worthy of note. The account he provides of articulation and conversation is of a potentiality realized, or at least partially so. The normative status that he accords this model results from its capturing our capacity to better grasp our character as language animals, to better understand and employ the capacity we have as such creatures. The crucial, initial enhancement of insight into this potential, as Taylor frequently stresses, came with romanticism and its new account of expressive meaning. Although many today reject the details of various romantic theories, Taylor would claim that at some level "we have all in fact become followers of the expressive view" that "has brought language more and more to centre stage . . . as the indispensable medium without which our typically human capacities, emotions, relations would not be." And, as this quality of the medium moves to center stage, so also has the increasing awareness that our relation to it is not one of controller-controlled. One reason for our intense fascination with language in the twentieth century is that we can't seem to unravel fully the open, uncertain, mysterious quality of our engagement with it.[39] Taylor's foregrounding of this quality in his accounts of articulation and conversation guarantees that his ontological insights, whether relating to templates or full constellations, signal their own limits, contain their own sense of contestedness; in short, they offer themselves as "weak" in my sense. Iron-

[38] "Comparison, History, Truth," 151, 159–64.

[39] "Language and Human Nature," 235–36. In speaking here of language, Taylor includes other symbolic forms as well, such as music and dance.

ically, then, the vestige of Hegelianism that attaches to Taylor's use of potentiality here is at the same time the vehicle for deflating more robust figures of thought that emerge from that legacy and are more closed to the challenge of otherness.

Some critics might reject this defense of Taylor on the grounds of his adamant antipathy for thinkers such as Foucault and Derrida. Taylor's hostility here might be taken as evidence of an unwillingness to listen to radically different perspectives, especially when the perspectives at issue are precisely ones that draw our attention to the way conversations may have hegemonic silences or may be drawn into certain paths rather than others simply through the subtle force of dominant discursive formations. One might conclude, accordingly, that Taylor's model of conversation is defective; it simply does not do an adequate job of signaling its own limits.

There is good reason to wonder at the rigidity of Taylor's opposition to some poststructuralist and postmodernist thought. On the one hand, Taylor has, over the years, offered plausible, specific critiques of such thought; for example, of Foucault's difficulties with normative political direction.[40] And yet, on the other hand, the extent of his antipathy seems to run beyond the point that would be justified by these arguments. Does this difficulty then count as evidence that Taylor's model of conversation is intrinsically flawed?

I want to resist this particular conclusion, without at the same time brushing aside the concern. Taylor has indeed, it seems to me, overlooked the way in which certain disruptive modes of reflection, such as genealogy and deconstruction, provide leavening strategies that could become useful components of his own model of conversation. But his failure here does not emerge directly from the model. It is rather rooted in a deep conviction about a certain danger that he sees adhering to the projects of at least some who follow in Nietzsche's wake. Thus the appropriate place to engage Taylor is on how well this crucial conviction can be justified. I will suggest that it is not as well supported as he thinks; before making this argument, however, I need to flesh out more extensively the character of his theism.

3.2. Theism and the Aesthetic-Expressive Dimension

Up to this point, all of Taylor's claims that I have examined can plausibly be interpreted in a weak ontological fashion. Things become more complex when one directly confronts his affirmation of theism. Readers of *Sources of the Self* are likely to end up somewhat concerned about the

[40] "Foucault on Freedom and Truth," *Political Theory* 12, no. 2 (1984).

tension that seems necessarily to arise between Taylor's portrait and affirmation of the *diversity* of modern moral sources, on the one hand, and his belief, stressed at the book's conclusion, that *one* such source, the Christian God of *agapé,* is the only "adequate" alternative, on the other.[41] Although Taylor emphasizes that he is uncertain about his ability to make this belief convincing, it is difficult for the reader not to feel that the earlier talk of diversity is somehow drained of its force.[42] The strong ontological trump card may still be held close to the vest, but its potential to sweep the game seems palpable.

In this section, I want to explore some reasons for resisting such a reading of Taylor. Toward this end, I will examine more closely his presentation of the third, modern ontological constellation that arises out of the expressivism of the Romantics (section 3.2.A). Although Taylor ultimately sides with the first, theistic constellation, the precise meaning of this affirmation has to be taken in light of that other affirmation I noted earlier (section 3.1.B), that "we have all . . . become followers of the expressive view."[43] The historical articulation of this view—or, better, constellation of views—from the late eighteenth century until today has brought to full consciousness an aesthetic-expressive potentiality of human being that theism cannot simply deny.[44] A theism that grapples seriously with this issue will have no trump card to play vis-à-vis nontheistic weak ontologies. There simply are no trump cards in this game (section 3.2.B).

3.2.A. The Expressivist Epiphany

The rich historical tale that Taylor relates about the emergence and varied development of the expressivist constellation is one of the most fascinating aspects of *Sources.* But this interpretive story is interwoven of course with judgments of greater or lesser adequacy in ontological terms. Adequacy here refers, first, to fit with the general template of moral sources and to openness to the diversity of sources that defines modernity. A stronger sense of adequacy, however, also comes into play. At issue is not which ontological constellation is minimally acceptable, but rather which can demonstrate its superiority to the other acceptable competitors. Here Taylor tries to show that the most defensible position today is one that integrates certain elements of expressivism with theism. It is

[41] *SS,* 10, 432, 516–21.
[42] *SS,* 10–11, 499.
[43] *SS,* 235–36.
[44] *SS,* 312–13, 491–93.

important to keep these different senses of adequacy separate in order to understand just what Taylor's theism implies philosophically.

What Taylor calls the "Expressivist Turn" emerges as several different insights coalesce in the German Sturm und Drang writers and continue to develop through English and German romanticism. Collectively these insights begin to constitute a conceptual constellation distinguishable both from orthodox Christianity and the disengaged rationalism of the radical Enlightenment. In relation to the former, there emerges a growing attachment to nature as an order "conducing to the life and happiness of the sentient creatures which it contains."[45] Increasingly, there develops a sense that this order is a moral source in itself, whose power need no longer be conceptualized in terms of the Creator within Christianity. In tandem with this growing affinity for nature, there emerges the sense that it is through the feelings or aesthetic sensibility—as much as or more than through reason alone—that one becomes attuned to this new source.[46] Our affective and aesthetic capacities give us access to "an inner impulse or conviction which tells us of the importance of our own natural fulfillment and of solidarity with our fellow creatures in theirs. This is the voice of nature within us." And it is this "impulse of nature" that comes to play the role of a "substitute for [the] grace" of the God of Christianity. Not surprisingly, for proponents of expressivism contact with this source was something that was threatened by a posture of cold, disengaged reason.[47]

To think in terms of such an inner voice or impulse is simultaneously to bring expression to the center of human being. In "articulating what we find within us" we also make something manifest, bring something of nature to expression. Two distinctive qualities characterize this novel sense of expression. First, that which is brought to expression is not something that "was already fully formulated beforehand"; rather its very character is partially constituted by the expression. Second, this curious quality of creating/discovering pertains both to that "élan running through the world" and to the being who is articulating it.[48]

This expressivist turn, which finds its moral source in the goodness of nature, goes through a variety of transformations in the nineteenth and twentieth centuries. As Taylor picks his way through this array of modifications, his primary concern is focused around two ontological axes, in terms of which he measures continuity and change: first, in a given manifestation of expressivism, *what* is it exactly that *is being expressed;* and,

[45] *SS,* 315.
[46] *SS,* 282–84, 294–302.
[47] *SS,* 369–70, 411.
[48] *SS,* 373–75.

second, is the expressivism still tied to a moral source, and is that source still conceived as *good?* In elucidating these issues, I want to start with what Taylor sees as the most challenging deviations that appear in the expressivist constellation, and then consider the continuities he finds. It is within the currents of the latter that he discerns alternatives worthy of affirmation today.

From the very start, the expressivist emphasis on inwardness and the creative imagination set up the conditions for later tension between the idea of an external order as the moral source, on the one hand, and the idea that the human self alone can become the pure center and measure of all that is around it. This is most clearly seen in that drift in much modernist art and literature through which aesthetic sensibility and its created objects come to claim for themselves an autotelic status. The "what" of expression collapses thereby into *self*-expression, and, correspondingly, the moral source becomes identified with the "powers of the self."[49]

A parallel deviation from the original forms of expressivism occurs as the assumption of the goodness of nature begins to come into question. Schopenhauer is a pivotal figure here for Taylor; after him, the way is open to a new range of views—from Nietzsche to Joseph Conrad—in which the "great current of nature" is reconceived as "vast, unfathomable, alien and amoral."[50] This shift allows for new expressivist options in which the source is still external or beyond human, but it is no longer a moral one, at least in as straightforward a sense as in theism or the original variants of expressivism.

Along with these deviations from the initial commitments of expressivism, there have also been continuities. Here Taylor is especially concerned to show how, in certain strands of modernist literature and poetry, the central idea of an "epiphany" has been retained. Taylor uses this term to capture

> the notion of a work of art as the locus of a manifestation which brings us into the presence of something which is otherwise inaccessible, and which is of the highest moral or spiritual significance; a manifestation moreover, which also defines or completes something, even as it reveals.[51]

Although Taylor wants to persuade us of expressivist continuity through this epiphantic experience, he is well aware that this kind of experience has been reconceptualized substantially in the twentieth century. He refers to the earlier romantic conception as an "epiphany of

[49] *SS*, 490.

[50] *SS*, 417, 441 ff.

[51] *SS*, 419. Taylor says that he borrows from and modifies James Joyce's use of this term.

being," in the sense that through artistic expression the goodness of being was to be intensely experienced. This is largely replaced in the twentieth century by the idea of an "epiphany of interspaces" or a "framing epiphany." Here the sense of being or nature as intrinsically and clearly characterized by good purpose has fallen away; accordingly, the epiphantic experience can no longer plausibly be comprehended as *expressing* such *purpose.* But that does not reduce the experience to a radically subjectivized one: "the great works of modernism," Taylor asserts, "resist our understanding them in a subjectivized fashion, as mere expressions of feeling or as ways of ordering the emotions."[52] Such works are rather concerned with some "transaction between ourselves and the world," some fashion in which the aesthetic object creates a frame or space that brings to presence some "forces" or qualities of "the order in which we are set." What such works keep open then is the exploration of the beyond human, the domain of external moral sources. Taylor sees such exploration at work in modern figures as diverse as Mann, Rilke, Ezra Pound, and D. H. Lawrence.[53]

Thus, the distinctiveness of the framing epiphany is manifested in its both bringing something beyond human to presence and yet no longer being fully expressive in the older sense, since the aesthetic experience does not clearly express some larger purpose. Moreover, this epiphany still gives a pronounced role to subjective expression, for now the "moral or spiritual order of things must come to us indexed to a personal vision" that is articulated in language or other symbolic forms. In other words, "the search for moral sources *outside* the subject" proceeds only "through languages that resonate *within* him or her."[54]

Clearly what attracts Taylor to those writers, philosophers, and poets who share this idea of epiphany is how they make central to human being moments of intense mutual vivification between an intensified subjectivity and sources external to it. Expressivism always emphasized the peculiar process of creating/discovering, as I noted earlier; but now the role of creativity is even more enhanced. Our expressive powers increasingly become essential to the "efficacy" of external sources. This extends finally to the very idea of "transfiguration" or "transmutation," the notion that aesthetic sensibility can be engaged to help redeem in some way a "despiritualized reality."[55] This conviction has, of course, taken a variety of forms. Some bind themselves to the theistic constellation of Christianity, such as Dostoyevsky or Rilke; others stay radically at a distance, as is

[52] *SS,* 474–76, 490–91.
[53] *SS,* 477, 482, 510.
[54] *SS,* 428, 510.
[55] *SS,* 446, 482.

the case with Nietzsche's notion of affirming the world. Despite these differences, however, their emphases on transfiguration are responses to that "crisis of affirmation" which arises as conviction of the innate goodness of things wanes in the nineteenth and twentieth centuries. In these responses, we see "the development of a human analogue to God's seeing things as good: a seeing which also helps effect what it sees."[56]

I will return shortly to this specific question of the affirmation of the goodness of being. For the moment, however, I want to reengage the question with which I started this section: what exactly does Taylor, as a proponent of theism, find to affirm within expressivism? The answer takes us back to the idea of a realized human potentiality for linguistic or symbolic articulation. In effect, Taylor is saying that our modern experience of expressivism offers certain insights that theism today must integrate. Accordingly, theists must understand that there is simply no immaculately uncontextualized "nugget of transcendent truth." In general, "our sense of the certainty or problematicity of God is relative to our sense of moral sources." What this means more specifically in relation to the expressivist constellation is that God as a moral source is now inextricably entangled with subjective articulation. Referring to this "interweaving of the subjective and transcendent," Taylor says that theology is "indexed" to "languages of personal resonance."[57]

3.2.B. A Weak Ontological Theism

Given this acceptance of a core element from expressivism, it becomes difficult to see how Taylor's theism could interpret itself as capable of deploying a strong ontological trump card. No religious tradition or individual belief can legitimately carry such force into the space of Taylorean articulation and conversation. There is no royal route that cuts through others; there is only the work of mutual interpretation and articulation of moral sources, in the context of which my arguments may finally resonate with you or not.

Thus, the suspicious secular reader of Taylor must, it seems to me, take him at his word in *Sources.* His claim is that the "major point" of the book is to elucidate our modern predicament as one in which three ontological constellations compete with one another, *and* in which resolutions of this predicament that try to succeed by conjuring away its constitutive terms are simply failures from the start. Such failures may come in the form of a utilitarianism that denies the very idea of moral sources or in

[56] *SS,* 448–49. The relevant biblical reference is to Genesis 1.

[57] *SS,* 312, 491–92, 512–13; and "Reply to Commentators," in a symposium on *Sources of the Self* in *Philosophy and Phenomenological Research* 54, no. 1 (1994): 211.

the form of a theism that finds its full bearings solely from some immaculately authoritative commands of God.[58] Each betrays a kind of willful blindness that marks it as inadequate in the sense either of ignoring "inescapable" ontological issues or of failing to do justice to the full range of problems and potentialities that are entangled with modern identity.

Understood in this fashion, the primary normative point of *Sources* is not that theism is best, but rather that certain ontological qualities and a certain range of sensitivity are necessary components in arguments about the modern self and its predicament. One could also say of such a claim that it broadly supports the idea of weak ontology. By this I mean that Taylor's claims about the three ontological constellations and how each must understand itself and its respective others accord reasonably well with the criteria I have laid out for weak ontological reflection. For my purposes, the especially interesting contribution Taylor makes is to delineate a theism that is no longer explicitly or implicitly tied to strong ontological claims. He shows persuasively that, regardless of whether one embraces theism or is thoroughly secular, the space of late modern conversation is such that no one can play strong ontological trump cards.

None of this means, however, that Taylor forgoes arguments aimed at defending a specific ontological constellation as the best. These arguments are crucial to him. Their force and urgency emerge from their role as basic articulations of the theistic moral source he affirms. But within the weak-ontological, conversational space of modernity, this force and urgency are perverted if they are understood as pure evidence of truth. Their proper role in this context has to do with motivation: inspiring one to a love of, and care for, conversational engagement and the commitment to interpretive work that it requires.

If we turn to the specific, substantive arguments that Taylor articulates in support of his own weak ontology, the paramount concern revolves around the *goodness* of moral sources. Here I first want to consider how Taylor squares off against the second modern ontological tradition, that rooted in the Enlightenment; in particular, what arguments does he marshal against utilitarianism, liberalism, and Deweyan social theory (at least in the form Rorty gives it). After briefly surveying these contests, I will turn back to the relationship of Taylor's theism to the expressivist ontological tradition. As I have shown, he draws deeply from this tradition; and yet it is also from this direction that he sees the most disturbing challenge emerging, more specifically in the form of Nietzsche.

Utilitarianism does not really enter the contest over which is the most adequate ontology. As shown earlier, it does not meet the first set of criteria of adequacy for philosophical frameworks Taylor establishes; in

[58] *SS*, 312, 512, 520.

short, it does not even fit onto the ontological template. It typically draws upon a moral source, but it does so implicitly, in a fashion that cannot be comprehended within the utilitarian framework that that source empowers (as shown in section 3.1.A). But one could certainly ask here: how might things change if that source were to be made more explicit? Taylor clearly finds the immediate prospects of such a shift to be dim. And that is because the source that utilitarianism implicitly trades upon is entangled in the radical Enlightenment's thorough rejection of religion in the name of "doing justice to the innocence of natural desire." Such an affirmation would make for a utilitarianism that is adequate to Taylor's ontological template, but how would its claim to be the best ontological account look? It would, Taylor asserts, remain deeply flawed. How can we today sustain a simple faith in the goodness of natural desire "in the face of our post-Schopenhauerian understanding of the murkier depths of human motivation?"[59]

A second family of perspectives Taylor calls procedural liberalism looks to no external source, be it nature or God.[60] Rather the moral source is the disengaged, rational autonomous self. Respect for that self drives moral consciousness and its construction of formal procedures to address suffering and do justice to all. What worries Taylor about this picture of human being and its world is the way it construes the experience of morality. Morality is felt primarily as a rational command to act across the gulf of disengagement and only minimally as an affirmation of others. Taylor thinks that such a "proceduralist meta-ethics" will ultimately prove inadequate to the task of sustaining a strong commitment to our modern ethical standards of benevolence and justice. "High standards need strong sources." And when the latter are reduced to the bare idea of disengaged, autonomous selves, to whom we owe respect, then the former will suffer. An emphatic reaffirmation of these standards can be elicited, Taylor argues, only on the basis of a moral source whose "central promise [is] a divine affirmation of the human" *(agapé)* that is "more total than humans can ever attain unaided."[61]

Taylor is of course aware that these arguments for the superiority of an ontology rooted in theism do not carry any knockdown power. I think his main purpose is merely to shift the burden of argument a bit against procedural liberalism, to challenge its hegemonic self-certainty. Taylor's challenge is perhaps strongest on the point of benevolence; more specifically whether it can be adequately motivated by secular respect for rational, autonomous selves.

[59] *SS*, 516–18; "Cross Purposes," 186 ff., 202.

[60] *POR*, 56–57.

[61] *SS*, 85–86, 516–18, 520–21.

But those proponents of proceduralism who call themselves "political liberals" might be willing to concede this point. They would argue, however, that at least when it comes to matters of justice, one does not need any ontology, whether it be tied to theism or the autonomous self. The justness of the procedurally fair, neutral liberal state can be established in a fashion that keeps all ontology at arm's length. This issue is, of course, important for the whole topic of weak ontology. I will pursue it further in chapter 5. For the moment I want to continue to consider conceptions of liberalism that would affirm some sort of ontological source.

A particularly interesting challenge to Taylor from within the second ontological constellation has been articulated by Richard Rorty. He affirms procedural liberalism generally, but he also draws upon the ideas of John Dewey in a fashion that promises more ontological carrying capacity. Rorty accepts Taylor's account of the inextricability of the concepts of agency and moral source. But he sketches an alternative view whose source is not external and yet has a greater capacity to empower than the bare idea of the rational, disengaged self. Specifically, we can affirm John Dewey's ideal of radical social imagination and hope, interpreting it now as a moral source. This scheme would, Rorty argues, fit quite plausibly both on Taylor's ontological template and into that second modern constellation, naturalism. This option would be an ontologically "*non*-reductive naturalism."[62] Central here would be the notion that we come to receive inspiration and empowerment as we articulate a vision we have collectively imagined of a "Social Democratic Future."[63] This source in no sense "reflects" something like *the* human predicament; it is, rather, grounded solely in the exercise of our capacity to hope, imagine, and will.

Rorty's reflections here touch upon an extremely important point, namely, how we decide what exactly counts as an acceptable weak ontology. Is Rorty mistaken about the Deweyean position fitting onto the weak ontological template? Or is he correct, thereby revealing that Taylor's arguments concerning external moral sources are actually structured more by his advocacy of theism than by his interpretive efforts to illuminate the boundaries of all that could plausibly count as weak ontology? In response to Rorty's challenge, Taylor attempts to explain exactly why the Deweyean alternative does not really count as an acceptable ontology. The reason is that its would-be moral source is reducible finally to a collective human projection. The ideal is in no way rooted in an "order

[62] Richard Rorty, "Taylor on Self-Celebration and Gratitude," *Philosophy and Phenomenological Research* 54, no. 1 (1994): 199. For Taylor's critique of naturalism's "reductive ontology," see *SS*, 337, 495.

[63] Rorty, "Taylor on Self-Celebration," 19.

in which we are set"; in other words, one not entirely of our choosing. Taylor clarifies this problem with Rorty's position by contrasting it with another one that is radically secular and antimetaphysical but would nevertheless fit the ontological template. Here he refers us again to Camus's Dr. Rieux in *The Plague,* in which we are presented with an ethic that preserves

> a moment of the recognition of something which is not made or decided by human beings, and which shows a certain way of being to be good and admirable. This may be nothing beyond the disenchanted universe which is the human predicament along with the human potentiality to respond the way Dr. Rieux does. But we recognize that *we have created neither this world nor this range of human capacities.* What remains open to us is to respond to this or not. But here we experience the choice not as one in which we might confer on this predicament its inspiring character, but rather it is a matter of whether we see it as truly moving. If we find ourselves forced to concede that it is, then there is no further role for the will beyond that of letting ourselves be moved by it.[64]

As Taylor sketches how the foregoing would count as weak ontology and Rorty's alternative would not, he illuminates an issue related to any sort of talk of criteria in such matters. In both my general discussion in chapter 1, as well as in Taylor's arguments in *Sources,* the very sense of ontological reflection today has been tied up with historical-interpretive judgments about the costs of the culture of modern subjectivity; more specifically, the effects of its disengagement from, and instrumental objectification of, its world. This means that what is allowed to count as a weak ontology cannot be divorced entirely from a pragmatic judgment as to whether a given alternative—say, Rorty's—generates enough critical distance from modern subjectivity and its typical blindnesses. Rorty shows a very precise sensitivity to this issue. Although he would like to think that his Deweyean perspective could generate such critical distance without an external moral source, he is honest enough to admit that the broad heritage of social democratic thought is deeply entangled in the "temptation" of arrogant, collective "self-celebration." In regard to this pragmatic judgment of adequate distance, he concludes: Taylor "may be right."[65] This admission is rather remarkable from someone who is renowned for countering any talk of transcendence with therapeutic advice to stop scratching what are really just imaginary itches. Rorty is not, of course, giving away the whole game to Taylor just yet; but he is recognizing just how distinctive and defensible an ontological position Taylor

[64] "Reply to Commentators," 212.

[65] Rorty, "Taylor on Self-Celebration," 200.

has developed. Rorty has thus, unlike many others, listened very carefully and not been drawn to inappropriate assessments by simple labels like "Christian and . . . Hegelian."

Taylor's response to Rorty would not be one of rejecting all ideas of social transformation in pursuit of modern life goods; his perspective would in fact support some goals of this sort. His suspicion rather would likely take the form of contending that strong appeals to utopian social imagination will generate significant dangers, if they are not linked to the articulation of an external moral source that in turn engenders a continual vivification of a sense of finitude and humility.

I want to turn now to the third ontological constellation, more particularly to the challenge of Nietzsche. Nietzscheans (or at least some of them) affirm a source external to human being, but it is an *amoral* source. For them, the heart of things is an unfathomable, purposeless presencing of life. What unsettles Taylor most deeply about such an ontological configuration is that Nietzsche joins it with a rejection of the modern life goods of benevolence and justice, something he sees as necessary to wean us away from a costly moral rigorism that too often follows from ethical commitment, especially when it is powered by a conviction that one is fulfilling God's purposes. Although Taylor admires Nietzsche's emphasis on affirming and transfiguring the world, he ultimately finds it to be unsatisfactory, since it has lost any footing in a commitment to others; in effect, the affirmation of the world is ethically idle. Consequently, Nietzsche offers us a "cruel dilemma": either affirmation without benevolence or benevolence with moral rigorism.[66] Taylor, of course, wants to convince us that we need not accept these terms of choice.

If Nietzsche does indeed present us with precisely the dilemma Taylor attributes to him, then a certain kind of theism looks more attractive. But, of course, the fascinating question that now hovers in the background is whether one can develop a weak ontology that might accept something like Nietzsche's external, amoral source and yet find a way of articulating it in a more life good–friendly fashion. If one developed an ethical orientation consonant with such an interpretation of sources, then it would constitute a powerful competitor on Taylor's own terms.

It is difficult to read the conclusion of *Sources* and not feel that Taylor deeply discounts the likelihood of such a challenge being successful. Arguments for this discounting are not really made explicit there, but a high degree of confidence seems present. The reasons behind this confidence become somewhat clearer in later essays. There he argues that thinkers like Nietzsche and Foucault represent a kind of "immanent counter-Enlightenment." This description is meant to capture two fea-

[66] *SS*, 455.

tures of their legacy. First, they question, as we have seen, the Enlightenment's assertion of the primacy of human flourishing expressed in the affirmation of benevolence and justice. Second, this primacy is not decentered by transcendence in the theistic sense, but rather by an *immanent* transcendence in which the "locus of death" comes to provide "in some sense a privileged perspective, the paradigm gathering point for life." Although this urge to immanent transcendence has taken a variety of forms, Nietzsche and the neo-Nietzscheans seem to be Taylor's main antagonists.[67] In *Sources,* these antagonists were indicted only on the count of having disengaged from central modern life goods. Here, however, Taylor deepens the critique and thereby lays bare the roots of that strong antipathy toward such thinkers that I touched upon earlier. He argues that when an emphasis is laid upon human finitude, and this is not in turn connected to a source that is good but rather amoral, the result is a peculiar "fascination with death and suffering" that finally cannot "escape the draw towards violence." This draw may manifest itself in different ways. Nietzsche expresses it through his attachment to a pre-Socratic kind of warrior ethic, within which risking death is the paradigm experience of life; Foucault expresses it in his fascination with transgression and "limit" experiences.[68]

We can see now the heart of Taylor's concern when it comes to a weak ontology's affirmation of external sources that are understood in amoral terms. In one sense, they serve a curious positive role for theism today, because they are a perpetual embarrassment to the legacy of the radically secular Enlightenment: they testify to "an ineradicable bent to respond to something beyond life."[69] They are, however, also profoundly dangerous, because their construal of this "bent" brings with it a fascination with violence.

It is hard not to read this as a fatal judgment. Others have certainly made similar pronouncements before. But is Taylor really entitled to make this determination with such apparent finality? Here it is instructive to turn to his own response to critics who assail Christianity and other religions for their history of intolerance and violence. Such critics, Taylor replies, "take the self-destructive consequences of a spiritual aspiration as a refutation of this aspiration." The fact that a theistic moral source has involved violence historically does not necessarily invalidate it, especially

[67] "The Immanent Counter-Enlightenment," paper presented to Castelgandolfo Colloquium VII, August 1996. Taylor mentions here various thinkers who fall into this category: Sartre, Camus, Derrida, Mallarmé, as well as Heidegger, at least as manifested in his early analysis of "Sein-zum-Tode" (7–12). See also "Spirituality of Life and Its Shadow," *Compass* 14 no. 2 (1996).

[68] "The Immanent Counter-Enlightenment," 12, 15.

[69] Ibid., 14.

when the alternative of a "stripped-down secular outlook" with no opening to external sources involves its own sort of self-mutilation: "stifling the response in us to some of the deepest and most powerful spiritual aspirations that humans have conceived." Since either alternative thus bears its own heavy burden, there is no easy choice. The theistic view can only be embraced with a deep sense of the challenge of overcoming "the terrible record of its adherents in history."[70]

But having situated his commitment to theism in this fashion, can Taylor so categorically pass judgment on those who would embrace some variant of a Nietzschean, external source? I don't think so. His concern with this tradition's "draw" toward violence has to be construed as a challenge to it, not a final sentence. Taylor stands to the Nietzscheans as his secular critics stand to him.

Kateb's ontology certainly affirms an external but amoral source. It would thus seem to qualify as a target for Taylor's critique. But it might be that Taylor would withhold his negative judgment here, since Kateb only draws partially upon Nietzsche. Taylor's claim might be more appropriately tested by applying it to those who embrace more fully the weight of the tradition running from Nietzsche to Foucault. This question will be pressed in the next two chapters, especially chapter 5.

3.3. Prefiguring the Political

In the process of elaborating Taylor's ontology, I have already indicated the way in which it aligns itself with some basic ethical-political values such as tolerance, reconciliation, conversation, and care. I want to turn now in a more sustained way to the question of the relationship between his ontology and his political theory. My intention is to show that Taylor's understanding of this relationship largely fits the pattern appropriate to weak ontology that I have called prefiguration. In this view an ontology is not like a treasure chest we discover after deep diving that contains a cache of "first things" inscribed with incontestable political directions. A weak ontology only prefigures ethical-political perception and judgment; that is, it focuses our attention cognitively and orients us affectively. And even this process is not a simple one-way avenue. One's perceptions and judgments can cohere into broad historical interpretations—most notably, regarding the character and prospects of late modernity—that in turn exert a constitutive pull on the character of one's ontology. What we problematize at this historical-interpretive level will deeply orient our ontological reflection.

[70] Ibid., 519–21.

In what follows I want to show that thinking in terms of the notion of prefiguration can help clarify Taylor's understanding of the connection between his ontological claims and his well-known affirmation, in "The Politics of Recognition," of a particular model of politics. Michael Walzer has referred to this as "liberalism$_2$," as distinct from the more familiar procedural notion of "liberalism$_1$." I will follow Walzer's usage.[71]

According to Taylor, a felicitous ontological claim does not so much legitimate categorically some alternative model of politics as it helps redraw "the map of political possibilities" that is imagined by liberalism$_1$.[72] Certain features on this map are taken to be relatively fixed, such as the modern welfare state and market economy. But within that general space of consensus, Taylor suggests, ontological reflection may vivify for us that there are "different ways of living the . . . structures that the contemporary age makes mandatory."[73]

Before turning directly to a sketch of liberalism$_2$, it is necessary to flesh out briefly one additional ontological thesis Taylor propounds. He argues that we cannot account adequately for social life if we stick to a strictly "atomistic" ontology, within which language and culture are conceived as only instrumentally related to the ultimate entities of society, individuals. This relation is, rather, at least partially constitutive, which means in turn that the good of culture is of a different kind than, say, the good of a highway. The latter acquires its goodness because it is instrumental in satisfying an aggregated set of desires of a discrete group of individuals. The former sort of good, on the other hand, is "irreducibly social" or "common." The good of a highway is merely a "convergent" sort of good.[74] The former sort can be related to an individual in a constitutive, nonsubstitutable way; the latter is instrumental to individual desires and functionally replaceable by any other convergent good that equally satisfies those desires. Thus an effective mass transit system might be substituted relatively easily for the highway. But in the case of a culture that is constitutively related to the identity of a social group, there is no wholesale functional equivalent. Its goodness has a rootedness in that group's way of life that make claims about its essential value stronger than similar claims about some given convergent good.

Taylor's argument here about a necessary, "holist" quality of some social goods belongs on the same level as the argument about certain "transcendental" features of moral life that I took up earlier (this is the first level of ontological reflection that I distinguished in section 3.1.A). Both

[71] See Walzer, "Comment," in *POR,* 99.

[72] *PA,* 202.

[73] *PA,* xii.

[74] *PA,* 136–39.

are template conceptualizations of the fundamental embeddedness of human being. But neither, by itself, settles any crucial moral or political controversies.

What the insight about irreducibly common goods does do, however, is refigure our perception of a polity that strongly affirms in its public policy the protection of the good of the "survival and flourishing" of a culture.[75] This refiguration decenters individual freedom somewhat, in the sense that its value in political life no longer has the kind of automatic, exclusive priority it has sometimes had within procedural liberalism. In effect, Taylor's ontological claim shifts the burden of argument in relation to procedural liberalism so that its relative inattention to the good of a flourishing culture becomes quite significant in ethical-political terms. A claim that living in this particular culture and community is essential to my identity now takes on a new, potential legitimacy; it may now be seen not as an irritating refusal to abandon premodern or antimodern modes of consciousness but rather as a plausible plea regarding an alternative way of "living the . . . structures" of modern life.

Such a sense of prefiguration allows us a better appreciation of "modern linguistic and cultural nationalism," as, for example, in Quebec.[76] Here, however, the mainstream liberal will of course raise the question as to how Taylor can guard against this appreciation turning into a legitimation of all sorts of denials of individual freedoms carried out in the name of protecting the cultural community. In this regard Taylor has argued,

> One has to distinguish the fundamental liberties, those that should never be infringed and therefore ought to be unassailably entrenched, on the one hand, from privileges and immunities that are important, but that can be revoked or restricted for reasons of public policy—although one would need a strong reason to do this—on the other.[77]

My guess is that this distinction, as it is deployed in "The Politics of Recognition," would not be adequate to relieve liberal anxiety. For in that essay and in the ones that flesh out the notion of irreducibly common goods, it is not so clear what source exactly Taylor is drawing upon for his affirmation of individual autonomy that would be comparable to the one he draws upon for his affirmation of cultural flourishing. Thus, it is easy to suspect that the good of the latter will too effortlessly trump the good of the former. If one turns back to *Sources of the Self,* however,

[75] *PAP,* 251. Taylor suggests some other significant common goods of this sort, such as "participatory, citizen self-rule," 251–52.

[76] *PA,* 140.

[77] *POR,* 59.

there are in fact resources for addressing this question. There one finds the ontological prefiguration of the good of individual autonomy and thus for the affirmation of a category of basic rights with a special status vis-à-vis claims made in the name of cultural flourishing. This prefiguration is drawn from the way Taylor describes the ontological center of gravity in moral life: the process of articulating moral sources. As has been shown, Taylor contends that in the modern world this articulation must be understood as a process where discovering is entangled with creating.

By making creation central to articulation, Taylor gives individual reflection, judgment, and expression a value that is not easily trumpable. No collective body can legitimately claim complete authority to determine which substantive articulations of moral sources will have "personal resonance" for me. It is this notion that gives sense to Taylor's privileging of a category of fundamental liberties and allows him to feel justified in calling the model of politics he affirms—at least for a situation like Quebec's—a *liberal* model.

But doubt remains as to whether Taylor's model really warrants that title. Already before the publication of "The Politics of Recognition," Will Kymlicka had sketched a notion of liberalism that takes culture more seriously than liberalism_1, and yet still keeps the claims of culture tied to the highest, exclusive good of autonomy. Kymlicka has since elaborated this view further.[78] In effect, it accepts the social-ontological claim about irreducibly common goods and the social character of individual identity. The capacity of individuals to exercise their autonomy is, Kymlicka admits, constitutively tied to their having the symbolic background onditions of an integral culture. If these conditions are essential to individual autonomy, then a liberal state may engage in some actions to ensure that integrity, even though they go beyond the bounds of state neutrality envisioned within liberalism_1.[79] Given its attempt to occupy a position between the neutral view and Taylor, I will call Kymlicka's view $\text{liberalism}_{1.5}$.

In the present context, the power of $\text{liberalism}_{1.5}$ resides in its claim to remain truer to the core value of autonomy and yet allow for many of the kinds of culture-sensitive policies that Taylor justifies under liberalism_2. Moreover, Kymlicka would assert that in the cases where liberalism_2 goes *beyond* $\text{liberalism}_{1.5}$, in giving priority to claims of cultural integrity over individual autonomy, it loses its legitimacy. For example, in the case of

[78] Will Kymlicka, *Liberalism, Community, and Culture* (Oxford: Clarendon Press, 1989), and *Multicultural Citizenship: A Liberal Theory of Minority Rights* (Oxford: Clarendon Press, 1995).

[79] Kymlicka, *Multicultural Citizenship*, especially chap. 5.

Quebec, Kymlicka would allow for federal, Canadian modifications to help protect the integrity of francophone culture in that province. Although this sort of protection of a national minority from a dominant cultural majority is legitimate, the same is not true for restrictions that a cultural community, whether majority or minority, might desire to impose internally on its individual members.[80] Thus, Kymlicka's model would apparently prohibit some of what Quebec has legislated in relation to language and education. It would disallow the policy that requires francophone parents to send their children to French-speaking schools. The good of autonomy here would dictate that such parents have the choice to opt out of French-language education if they wish, perhaps because they perceive better economic opportunities for their children if they were to receive an English-language education.[81]

Taylor would, on the contrary, defend the Quebec education policy, arguing that it is a reasonable restriction on freedom, justified in the name of the common good of maintaining the integrity of francophone culture. He argues that thinkers like Kymlicka simply do not understand that it is legitimate to see autonomy and cultural integrity as "two independent goods."[82] Once we admit this, then the choice of a democratic majority to prefer the good of cultural integrity here is not automatically unjust. But again, this line of thought does not give blanket warrant to inroads on autonomy. Parents' right to educate their children is certainly fundamental; but the right of French-speaking parents in Quebec to choose education in a language other than French is not.

If one tries to determine exactly what is at the heart of Taylor's defense here, there seems to be something problematic about his explicit argument. He sometimes makes it seem as though the whole matter turns on whether one acknowledges the social-ontological claim about irreducibly common goods, as if such ontological acknowledgment somehow directly imparts moral legitimacy to his defense. And yet Taylor has himself cautioned against just such a jump in argumentation, as I noted above. Moreover, Kymlicka's model would seem to have in fact already coherently acknowledged the ontological point and yet drawn a different moral conclusion from Taylor.

Although Taylor might thus be interpreted as deploying a confused defense on this issue, I would argue that he has available a way of making his argument that accords better with the criteria of weak ontology. The

[80] See Kymlicka's distinction between legitimate efforts to provide "external protection" to a national minority and illegitimate efforts to put "internal restrictions" on the members of any cultural group, in ibid., 35–44, 104–5.

[81] Cf. the argument made by K. Anthony Appiah, "Identity, Authenticity, Survival: Multicultural Societies and Social Reproduction," in *POR*, 159–63.

[82] *PAP*, 251.

moral difference between liberalism$_2$ and liberalism$_{1.5}$ gains its significance for Taylor in the final analysis because of its prefiguration in the ontological and historical-interpretive claims developed in *Sources of the Self.*

The key question is simply why Taylor feels the need for the good of cultural integrity to be accorded such a high value vis-à-vis autonomy. The answer has to be sought, I think, in his claim about the ontological space of modern conversation; and, more particularly, about the necessity of maintaining space for "alternative modernities" within which the exploration of external moral sources is central. My guess here is that Taylor would contend that, all else being equal, the flourishing of such exploration is enhanced in societies where the polity can act, within limits, to enhance the congruence of the cultures within it and thereby honor "affiliations with some depth in time and commitment."[83]

It is important to understand just what is and is not being suggested here. Taylor's point is not that all the world should be refashioned in accordance with the model of liberalism$_2$. It is rather that a world that accords a legitimate place to societies that choose liberalism$_2$ will be one that does better justice to the depth of diversity that constitutes the ontological space of late modernity. Further, it is crucial to understand that such an ethical-political perspective on language and culture does not license wholesale drives to cultural insularity and hostility. Its rootedness in Taylor's accounts of late modernity and moral articulation prefigures a specific ethos of conversation, central to which is an orientation to listening and the interpretive work necessary to exploring the ontological space of our predicament.

[83] *SS,* 513.

Chapter Four

JUDITH BUTLER'S BEING-IN-TROUBLE

A GUIDING IMPERATIVE of Judith Butler's thought is the commitment to "a problematizing suspension of the ontological." Drawing upon the momentum of both feminist and poststructuralist thought, she understands her task to be an "interrogation of the construction and circulation" of ontological claims. By this, she means an investigation of the multitude of ways in which notions of being have traditionally been construed as "pre-linguistic" or "pre-given" and thus as having a kind of privileged, uncontestable status in accounts of subjectivity, society, and politics.[1] When an account is rooted in an "ontological essentialism" or "metaphysics of substance," Butler contends, there is an occlusion of power, for such ontology invariably contains a "normative injunction that operates insidiously by installing itself into political discourse as its necessary ground."[2] This allows categories of identity, for example gender, to present themselves as beyond contestation.

In the wake of Foucault, the deployment of philosophical efforts to expose power in inconspicuous places is, of course, familiar. But Butler's efforts display a number of characteristics that give it a real distinctiveness. For one thing, her unmasking operation unfolds through a perspective that goes a good bit beyond Foucault in its understanding of language and power. An analysis of this perspective and how it enables her critique of ontological essentialism, especially as it has appeared in feminism, will be my entry point for taking up the issue of Butler's own affirmation of an alternative ontology (section 4.1).

The following abbreviations will be used for referring to Butler's books:

BTM *Bodies That Matter: On the Discursive Limits of "Sex."* New York: Routledge, 1993.

ES *Excitable Speech: A Politics of the Performative.* New York: Routledge, 1997.

GT *Gender Trouble: Feminism and the Subversion of Identity.* New York: Routledge, 1990.

PLP *The Psychic Life of Power: Theories in Subjection.* Stanford, Calif.: Stanford University Press, 1997.

[1] Judith Butler, "The Force of Fantasy: Feminism, Mapplethorpe, and Discursive Excess," *Differences* 2 no. 2 (1990): 105–6.

[2] *GT,* 16, 20; *BTM,* 219.

Formally, this affirmation is announced when she asserts that foundations are both "contingent and indispensable."[3] This simple statement embodies, however, a persistent tension, one that frequently manifests itself in the work of poststructuralist and postmodern thinkers. Sometimes they deny the necessity of foundations altogether. But when indispensability is admitted, the affirmative task presents itself as immensely difficult. Its difficulty results, of course, from the very power and relentlessness of the critiques such theorists have offered of prior ontological formulations. Those critiques highlight the dangers residing in any attempt at affirmative gestures. The upshot, unsurprisingly, is a tendency to keep ontological affirmations austerely thin or minimal. Perhaps one might draw a very rough analogy here with Marx's refusal to say much about the normative qualities of communism. Such talk, he thought, ran the danger of becoming ideology. Thus, reticence or austerity of discourse began to look like a virtue. This is, of course, a view that appears a good bit more doubtful with hindsight.

I want to suggest that ontological *thinness* ought to be distinguished from ontological *weakness*. The former refers to a reticence to affirm very much ontologically; the latter to the way one affirms. The problem with the former is its failure either to figure enough existential universals or to sketch persuasively how the ontology prefigures ethical-political values. In my terms, a weak ontology that is too thin will not be very felicitous. A felicitous weak ontology has a kind of richness to it, with that term implying that the ontology satisfies the various criteria I have delineated. Just as with soups, so with weak ontologies: a rich one is usually more satisfying than a thin one.

One thing that makes Butler's work so fascinating is how these issues play themselves out in the development of her work after *Gender Trouble* (1990). The tension over ontological thinness—although obviously not framed in such terms—arises in the context of critiques of that volume. *Gender Trouble* unmasks the ontological essentialism at work in various different conceptualizations of subjectivity, gender, and the body. Butler's point is to expose ontological claims in these domains as nothing more than dissimulation strategies of discursive regimes of power. Despite the novelty of her way of conceiving the relation of power and language, critics have argued that her notion of subjectivity is so thoroughly embedded within the flows of power, that she (like Foucault) makes it impossible to imagine a subject having the capability of critical agency; that is, the wherewithal to turn against power.[4] Although Butler broaches

[3] Butler, "For a Careful Reading," in S. Benhabib, J. Butler, D. Cornell, and N. Fraser, *Feminist Contentions: A Philosophical Exchange* (New York: Routledge, 1995), 133.

[4] See, for example, Seyla Benhabib, "Feminism and Postmodernism," 20–21, and Nancy Fraser, "False Antitheses," 67–69, both in Benhabib et al., *Feminist Contentions*; Peter

this problem in *Gender Trouble,* it is only in succeeding reflections that she has treated it in a more adequate fashion. And as she has pursued this elaboration, her own counterontology has emerged (section 4.2).

After elucidating this initiative, I take up the question of Butler's tendency to join her acceptance of the indispensability of ontological foundations with a reticence to flesh hers out more—the problem of thinness. I show that this tendency yields some difficulties that show up both in how well the ontology prefigures her ethical-political values and in how well it figures the existential universal of finitude (section 4.3).

After pushing this issue of ontological reticence against Butler, I will conclude by backing off a bit. In her later work, *The Psychic Life of Power* (1997), there is an analysis of melancholia and mourning that, at first sight, might not seem to be immediately connected with ontological questions. But my extended complaint about thinness will help make the relevance clear. Butler's engagement with what might seem to be only a psychological topic constitutes in fact also a significant enrichment of her ontology; and it is an enrichment that provides finally a somewhat more satisfactory figuration of finitude (section 4.4).

4.1. Feminism and Foundations

An important focus of feminist critique in the last thirty years has been its attack on the traditional use of ontological categories to provide justifications for gender hierarchy. Male ways could appear accordingly as "natural" ways, not ones entangled with relations of power. This strategy for disrupting gender hierarchy led as well to various efforts to reevaluate the identity of women. These efforts have proven to be quite contentious, as each attempt to essentialize a core sense of identity has engendered in turn the response that it is in some important sense exclusionary; for example, in the 1980s, certain claims to speak in the name of all women were exposed to intense criticism for implicitly tying that identity to the experience of white, heterosexual, middle-class women of North America and Europe.

This dialectic of argument could, of course, be given various interpretations. One could see it as progressive, in the sense of moving toward some more adequate account of women, which in turn would provide an ontological anchor for an identity politics cohering around gender. On the contrary, one could contest this progressive image entirely, asserting instead that the search for any such ontological anchor is misguided. Each new possible anchor merely inconspicuously reinstalls a

Digeser, *Our Politics, Our Selves: Liberalism, Identity, and Harm* (Princeton, N.J.: Princeton University Press, 1995), chaps. 1 and 4; and Martha Nussbaum, "The Professor of Parody: The Hip, Defeatist Feminism of Judith Butler," *New Republic,* February 22, 1999, 42.

novel arrangement of power. But this interpretation has had a deeply disturbing resonance for feminist politics, because it now becomes unclear what precisely is distinctive about such a project, and around what exactly its solidarity is to be formed. Accordingly, this interpretation has engendered, as Butler puts it, a recurrent "sense of trouble." The loss of the possibility of an ontologically secured, deep identity is deeply unsettling. But rather than struggle against the force of this insight, we should embrace it and acknowledge that "trouble is inevitable."[5] Ontologically expressed, one might say that, for Butler, human being just is *being-in-trouble,* with this term having a rough parallel to the early Heidegger's description of human being as *Sein-zum-Tode* (being-toward-death).[6] In Butler's terms, human being is constituted in "terms that are never fully one's own."[7]

As a result of this view, Butler has been determined to foil any attempt by feminists or gay and lesbian theorists to find some anchor of identity, some ontological "terms of one's own." One way in which she has done this is to upset the understanding some feminists have had of the distinction between sex and gender. In this understanding, gender is culturally constructed and thus is the site where patriarchal power instantiates itself. Sex, on the other hand, in the sense of the male and female bodies, is not socially constructed. Crudely stated, gender is to culture as sex is to nature. The sexed body is thus cast into a prediscursive realm, which in turn functions as the ontological well at the bottom of which one seeks the identity of woman. Of course, this going to the ontological well is intended to serve emancipatory, feminist goals rather than patriarchal ones. Such is the intention, for example, of Julia Kristeva's appeal to "maternal instinct" or Monique Wittig's appeal to the "lesbian body."[8] However understandable such intentions may be, Butler contends that this kind of strategy is always doomed from the start. There simply are no prediscursive ontological sites on which to rest identity and politics. The idea of such a site is always a conceptualization; conceptualization is always embedded in discursive contexts; and discourse is always entangled with power. Butler even presses this insight upon the master himself: Foucault, when he appealed to "bodies and pleasures" as the substantive site of resistance-beyond-power, was succumbing to the illusory attractions of the ontological well.[9]

[5] *GT,* vii.

[6] Martin Heidegger, *Being and Time,* trans. J. Macquarrie and E. Robinson (New York: Harper and Row, 1962), division 2, chap. 1.

[7] *PLP,* 28; *ES,* 26.

[8] *GT,* 6–7, 89–120.

[9] *GT,* 94–96.

In delineating the notion of weak ontology, I have referred to various efforts to conceive subjectivity as "stickier" than has been the case in predominant modern formulations. Butler, in effect, strongly radicalizes this idea: discourse does not "*mire* the subject," since there is no quality we could point to in order to secure the notion of subjectivity *prior* to discourse; rather, discourse thoroughly constitutes the subject. We must reconceptualize subjectivity, identity, and body as "*effect*[s], that is, as *produced* or *generated*."[10]

Butler gives this Foucauldian-inspired idea a novel sense in *Gender Trouble*. There, in trying to undermine the familiar "expressive model" of the sexed body and gender, in which the latter culturally expresses the prediscursive identity or essence of the former, she argues for the employment of a "performative" model. On this view

> words, acts, gestures, and desire produce the effect of an internal core or substance, but produce this *on* the surface of the body, through the play of signifying absences that suggest, but never reveal, the organizing principle of identity as a cause. Such acts, gestures, enactments, generally construed, are *performative* in the sense that the essence or identity that they otherwise purport to express are *fabrications* manufactured and sustained through corporeal signs and other discursive means. That the gendered body is performative suggests that it has no ontological status apart from the various acts which constitute its reality. This also suggests that if that reality is fabricated as an interior essence, that very interiority is an effect and function of a decidedly public and social discourse, the public regulation of fantasy through the surface politics of the body, the gender border control that differentiates inner from outer, and so institutes the "integrity" of the subject. In other words, acts and gestures, articulated and enacted desires create the illusion of an interior and organizing gender core, an illusion discursively maintained for the purposes of the regulation of sexuality within the obligatory frame of reproductive heterosexuality. If the "cause" of desire, gesture, and act can be localized within the "self" of the actor, then the political regulations and disciplinary practices which produce that ostensibly coherent gender are effectively displaced from view. The displacement of a political and discursive origin of gender identity onto a psychological "core" precludes an analysis of the political constitution of the gendered subject and its fabricated notions about the ineffable interiority of its sex or of its true identity.[11]

Although this performative model is introduced in *Gender Trouble* as part of Butler's specific critique of feminist theory, she clearly intends it

[10] *GT,* 143, 147.
[11] *GT,* 136.

to have the broadest possible philosophical implications. She is providing a way of understanding that there is no "doer behind the deed"; or rather that the "doer" is constituted by the "doing" of "signifying practices." Such practices instantiate discursive codes that themselves define what is to count as an intelligible, normal "doer" or subject. Such subjects take on their "substance" only through the regulated process of continual iteration. In this production of "substantializing effects" power is both exercised and concealed. It is concealed insofar as the subject comes to appear to have a substance that preexists the practices of signification, thus allowing it to seem to stand at a sovereign distance from the cultural terrain that it negotiates.[12]

One of the fascinating aspects of Butler's picture is the way in which she tries to avoid the dead end of what one might call the "discursive dope" image of subjectivity. If subjectivity is merely a production of discourse, one might ask, doesn't it lose all capacity for critical agency—become in effect a one-dimensional mouthpiece for reproducing discursive power? Such reproduction is never assured once and for all, according to Butler, for "discursive injunctions" are always liable to failure in ongoing practices of mundane signification.

> The injunction *to be* a given gender produces necessary failures, a variety of incoherent configurations that in their multiplicity exceed and defy the injunction by which they are generated. Further, the very injunction to be a given gender takes place through discursive routes: to be a good mother, to be a heterosexually desirable object, to be a fit worker, in sum, to signify a multiplicity of guarantees in response to a variety of different demands all at once. The coexistence or convergence of such discursive injunctions produces the possibility of a complex reconfiguration and redeployment.[13]

Thus signification and resignification always carry the possibility of critical variation or "subversive repetition." Again using the case of gender, Butler says that bodily surfaces that are pervasively enacted in ways that naturalize gendered identity can also become the site of a "dissonant and denaturalized performance" that can help reveal "the performative status of the natural itself": in short, its implication in the discursive regime of "compulsory heterosexuality." She illustrates this subversive possibility with the example of the cultural practice of "drag" or female impersonation. Such a practice subverts by parody the expressive model of gender and sexual identity by presenting conflicting pictures of true identity and its expression. On the one hand, the "true" inside seems

[12] *GT,* viii–ix, 142–45.
[13] *GT,* 145.

masculine while its outside expression is feminine; on the other hand, the actor seems to be asserting that, at another level, my really "true" inside is feminine but my bodily outside is masculine.[14] The existence of two contradictory truth claims here should suggest, Butler concludes, that the model of true expression is inappropriate; in effect, it does not capture a real relationship but rather helps conceal and reproduce power.

The sheer boldness of Butler's theoretical initiatives in *Gender Trouble* has, not surprisingly, elicited an array of critiques exposing what appear to be crucial faults. My present interest does not really lie in exploring these specific criticisms per se or in the particulars of Butler's response. However, it is in the further elucidation of her perspective under the pressure of these critiques that the shape of her alternative ontology has emerged more clearly than was the case in *Gender Trouble.*

4.2. "An Ontology of Present Participles"

If one characteristic of a plausible, weak ontological rendering of human being is an account of language that displaces the disengaged, sovereign conception of subjectivity, then Butler's ontology certainly can make this claim. But the very radicality of that displacement in *Gender Trouble* creates some difficulties. For one thing, the fact that human beings have bodies seems to have become somehow an epiphenomenon of performativity. Another problem is that it is not entirely clear how, specifically, discursive power "produces" subjects. Finally, although she provides an example of the way subjects can resist power in *Gender Trouble,* one can be skeptical as to whether her own theory in fact allows adequate comprehension of the critical agency she wishes to affirm. As I trace Butler's effort to wrestle with these problems, the contours of her alternative to a strong or essentialist, ontology will become apparent. Once these contours are visible, I can then better assess how well her thinking aligns itself with the other criteria of a felicitous weak ontology.

Reflecting upon her task regarding the constitution of the subject, Butler writes: "That one comes to 'be' through a dependency on the Other—an Hegelian and, indeed, Freudian postulation—must be recast in linguistic terms."[15] For this purpose, she finds useful an image employed by Louis Althusser to capture the idea of subjectivity being simultaneously constituted by power and given recognition. A policeman on a street yells "Hey you there!" and a passerby stops and turns in response,

[14] *GT,* 93, 124, 137, 146. Butler draws here on the insights of Esther Newton's *Mother Camp: Female Impersonators in America* (Chicago: University of Chicago Press, 1972.)

[15] *ES,* 26.

acknowledging the policeman's call. In this "interpellation," as Althusser calls it, the passerby is, in effect, "hailed" into being; he/she is officially accorded subjectivity and given recognition, but on power's own terms.[16]

The core of what fascinates Butler here is the idea of being "hailed" or "called" into social or "linguistic life."[17] But the constitutive process apparent in this image would seem to be less thoroughgoing than Butler herself demands. After all, don't we have a fully formed subject—the passerby—who enacts the turn to authority? Butler is amply aware that the example is limited in its heuristic value. What she says is that we cannot just think in terms of isolated scenes. Imagine rather a lifetime of being hailed into discourse, beginning with the doctor who announces: "It's a girl!" Keeping in mind the earlier analysis of gender as performative, Butler would have us reconstrue this familiar speech act as the beginning of a lifelong chain of "girling" utterances that enact certain scripts as normal and others as abnormal. With this expansion of the temporal horizon and application of the notion of performativity, the relatively sovereign subjectivity of the passerby begins to dissolve. It is replaced by the image of a subjectivity produced or constituted by the insistent, interpellating "demand" of "discursive power."[18]

Butler also departs from the literal sense of Althusser's scene in that she finds misleading the image of the call as a sovereign performance of the policeman. As with Foucault, she wishes to displace our propensity to seek a "who" that is responsible for discursive power. The felicity or success of the policeman's utterance does not proceed primarily from his will or intention, as J. L. Austin was aware, but rather from convention:

> The policeman who hails the person in the street is enabled to make that call through the force of reiterated convention. This is one of the speech acts that police perform, and the temporality of the act exceeds the time of the utterance in question. In a sense, the police cite the convention of hailing, participate in an utterance that is indifferent to the one who speaks it. The act "works" in part because of the citational dimension of the speech act, the historicity of convention that exceeds and enables the moment of its enunciation.[19]

[16] Louis Althusser, "Ideology and Ideological State Apparatuses (Notes towards an Investigation)," in *Lenin and Philosophy and Other Essays,* trans. B. Brewster (New York: Monthly Review Press, 1971).

[17] *BTM,* 121–24; *ES,* chap. 1; and *PLP,* chap. 1.

[18] *GT,* 145; *ES,* 34, 49, 155; Butler, "Performative Acts and Gender Constitution: An Essay in Phenomenology and Feminist Theory," in *Performing Feminisms,* ed. Sue-Ellen Case (Baltimore: Johns Hopkins University Press, 1991), 271. Butler speaks of a "demand to align oneself with the law" (*PLP,* 107).

[19] *ES,* 33.

Thus it is the reiterating function of language that is primarily carrying and reproducing dominant norms and creating the effect of sovereign, disengaged subjects by the continual process of calling them into social existence. We are, in short, "interpellated kinds of beings," continually being called into linguistic life, being "given over to social terms that are never fully [our] own."[20]

Butler's ontology then is one in which the basic "things" are persistent forces or processes. We must be careful not to imagine these as having qualities of subjectivity. Thus, power is not an anonymous *subject* that initiates discrete *acts* of constitution or construction. There is rather only "a process of reiteration by which both 'subjects' and 'acts' come to appear at all. There is no power that acts, only a reiterated acting that is power in its persistence."[21]

However overwhelming this world of power persisting, insisting, compelling, demanding, and hailing may sound, Butler does not think, as I noted in section 4.1, that any of this implies a notion that subjects are dopes of discursive power. Reiterating is always potentially open to resignifying in ways that may contest the smooth reproduction of the dominant terms of discourse. Butler has described this subversive potential as "power's own possibility of being reworked." Her point in employing such a curious locution is, of course, to keep us from refiguring subjectivity again into a form that is self-causing in its critical agency.[22] But, even when one follows this line of thinking sympathetically, what one is left with is simply the formal idea that discursive power reproduces itself imperfectly or unstably. The causes and occasions of this imperfect process are no doubt multiple. What is not yet clear in Butler's account is *why* or *how* this imperfection might ever be taken advantage of intentionally by an actor.[23] In her account of subject constitution so far, there is really nothing one could use for making much headway toward an answer. Before turning directly to the resources Butler develops for such an answer, I want to consider briefly how she has tried to respond to criticism of her account of the body. This is done in the context of a further augmentation of her "ontology of present participles."[24]

The criticism in its simplest version takes the form of questions like: if the body is really thoroughly a constitutive effect of some discourse, how is it that, regardless of the discourse that is prevalent at any given place

[20] *ES,* 26; *PLP,* 28.

[21] *BTM,* 9.

[22] Butler, "Contingent Foundations: Feminism and the Question of 'Postmodernism,' " in Benhabib et al., *Feminist Contentions,* 47; and *BTM,* 15. See Nancy Fraser's criticism of this expression in "False Antitheses," 67.

[23] Cf. Butler's definition of agency, *PLP,* 15.

[24] Butler, "Performative Acts," 272.

and time, I feel pain when colliding with a door frame? *What,* one asks, is colliding with that frame?[25]

In response to such objections, Butler, in *Bodies That Matter,* suggests:

> To claim that discourse is formative is not to claim that it originates, causes, or exhaustively composes that which it concedes; rather, it is to claim that there is no reference to a pure body which is not at the same time a further formation of that body. . . . In philosophical terms, the constative claim is always to some degree performative.
>
> . . . [T]o "refer" naively or directly to . . . an extra-discursive object will always require the prior delimitation of the extra-discursive. And insofar as the extra-discursive is delimited, it is formed by the very discourse from which it seeks to free itself.[26]

Butler's point then is not to collapse materiality into a linguistic idealism; but neither will she allow materiality to be ontologically posited in a fashion that places it firmly outside of language, because that very positing is itself accomplished in language. She tries to express this relation of language and materiality in her own ontological idiom as follows. We should figure the materiality of the body—manifesting itself in domains as varied as chemical composition, metabolism, illness, death—not as a passive medium, but rather as a persistent

> *demand in and for language,* a "that which" which prompts and occasions. . . . [W]ithin the cultural fabric of lived experience, [it calls to be] fed, exercised, mobilized, put to sleep, a site of enactments and passions of various kinds. To insist upon this demand, this site, as the "that without which" no psychic operation can proceed, but also as that on which and through which the psyche also operates, is to begin to circumscribe that which is invariably and persistently the psyche's site of operation; not the blank slate or passive medium upon which the psyche acts, but, rather, the constitutive demand that mobilizes psychic action from the start, that is that very mobilization, and, in its transmuted and projected bodily form, remains that psyche.[27]

The materiality of the body is a "referent" that is not fully capturable by language, but that takes its place in language as "an insistent call" to be attended to.[28] With this notion, Butler installs in her ontology a second site of insistence, alongside that of interpellation. The latter is an insistence that subjects *be* this or that and continually account for themselves.

[25] See Digeser, *Our Politics, Our Selves,* 153–56; Kathleen Jones, *Compassionate Authority: Democracy and the Representation of Women* (New York: Routledge, 1993), 79, 218; and Nussbaum, "The Professor of Parody," 36, 42.

[26] *BTM,* 10–11.

[27] *BTM,* 67.

[28] *BTM,* 67.

This additional site of insistence also pressures something toward intelligibility; but that something, materiality, is also conceived as always exceeding the grasp of language. Thus it seems curiously to be a force that aligns itself with discursive power insofar as it is responsible for the inexhaustibility of the latter's task. The force of interpellation will always be called forth anew, since the material referent of naming is always beyond its reach.

This postulation of a second ontological force extricates Butler from the anomalies of a linguistic idealism, but it does not seem to have augmented the overall ontological picture to a point where the emergent property of critical agency acquires adequate clarity. Progress on this front has come, though, in the context of Butler's recent efforts toward "thinking the theory of power together with a theory of the psyche."[29] Such a task is important to Butler for a couple of reasons. Not only can it help us better comprehend agency, it can also make clearer the phenomenon of submission in the constitution of the subject. Clearly subjectivation in Foucault's sense is productive (of agency and other things); but it also brings about a submission. What are the specific mechanisms of psychic life through which these effects occur?

In regard to the question of agency and resistance to power, psychoanalysis would seem to have a ready answer: resistance can be traced to some "internal" psychic force that is prior to, and thus in some sense beyond, "external" power. But Butler is wary of any simple positing of an ontologically distinct, inner sphere of "eternal psychic facts" that, in turn, tells us that some specific resistance to power is, as it were, built into being as necessary.[30]

Butler turns once more to Althusser's scene to open up this problematic terrain. What she finds unexplained in both Althusser and Foucault is why the passerby turns to answer the policeman. Power "hails," but why does one submit to its call? Any attempt to answer this question will of course be made more difficult by remembering that the process of turning here is also constitutive of subjectivity (recall again that Butler always wants us to depart from the image of an isolated scene and imagine the activity and effects of interpellation extended over a lifetime). There is, in short, no fully reflective subject who is choosing to submit. The submission Butler is seeking to explain precedes the reflective self; that is, the self with a conscience.

Drawing on both Freud and Nietzsche, Butler understands conscience as forming under the force of the prohibitions of power. Desire turns back upon itself in the form of a will in the service of a regulating regime,

[29] *PLP,* 3.
[30] *PLP,* 127–29.

that is, of terms not one's own. The resulting pain of self-denial and self-beratement is, however, compensated for, as Freud saw, by the investment of erotic energy in the prohibitive activity of this emergent entity of conscience. The conscience can thus never be an adequate site for thinking critical agency, since it is, in its very constitution, in complicity with the violent appropriation of desire by power.

A conceptualization of conscience in these terms helps to generate a sharper focus on the underlying issue of submission. A more precise phrasing of the question as to why the subject turns can now be offered: Why does desire cooperate with its own prohibition? Butler's answer rests on her postulation of a "desire to be" or "to persist" that characterizes human beings. This is not a desire for mere physical survival or to align with some metaphysical essence; it is rather the desire for *social* existence, *linguistic* survival. Moreover, this desire has as its "final aim" not some particular model of existence, but rather merely "the continuation of itself"; it is thus "a desire to desire." And this desire will cooperate with the prohibition of any particular desire that endangers its continued access to the terms of social existence. Here, then, is the psychic mechanism of submission: "the desire to desire is a willingness to desire precisely that which would foreclose desire, if only for the possibility of continuing to desire." One attaches to what is painful rather than not attach at all. This impulse, this passionate, "stubborn" propensity to attach is something that "precede[s] and condition[s] the formation of subjects."[31]

A moment ago, I indicated that Butler clarifies the notion of critical agency in the process of exploring the phenomenon of submission. But, having seen how deeply she roots submission in psychic life, it would seem she has only made the problem of thinking agency *more* difficult. This would appear to be true in two senses. First, given one's stubborn attachment to the dominant terms into which one has been interpellated, any resistance to them would mean risking a kind of social death. This is indeed what Butler wants to claim. A second sense in which the idea of critical agency becomes apparently more difficult is that one cannot see as yet any psychic mechanism by which there could even be such a space of possible experience. Stubborn attachment seems unshakable. Butler contends, however, that this is not the case. For if a regulatory regime is secured only as it calls forth and constitutes a desire for existence within a specific set of terms, it means that there is a certain "detachability of desire." Desire blocked or foreclosed can invest itself in

[31] *PLP*, 27–28, 61–62, 102, 130.

that very prohibition.[32] But with this capacity of desire there also comes a certain susceptibility of power.

> If desire has as its final aim the continuation of itself—and here one might link Hegel, Freud, and Foucault all back to Spinoza's conatus—then the capacity of desire to be withdrawn and to reattach will constitute something like the vulnerability of every strategy of subjection.[33]

In this moment of detachability there emerges that "formative and fabricating dimension of psychic life" in terms of which one can conceive a resistance to power that is capable not just of blind recalcitrance, but also a rearticulation of the dominant terms in which a specific form of social existence is offered.[34]

Critical agency, for Butler, thus seems to gain its condition of possibility from a "constitutive desire," the "desire to desire." This desire is, potentially, more stubborn, resourceful and opportunistic than the passionate attachment that forms the submissiveness of subjectivity. Butler figures this desire as a sort of insistent demand or becoming. Thus it appears to be of a kind with the other two ontological forces I have delineated. Each is a force in the sense of an insistence. None of them is an entity in the sense of being fully describable as subjects or objects. Power, materiality, and the desire to desire are thus all referents that "cannot be finally named."[35] The "it" of these forces is like the "it" of "it is raining."

Collectively these insistences configure that *turning* that so fascinates Butler and in the context of which subjectivity is engendered. But this configuration allows a space of variation. Not only can a normalized subject be engendered but also a critical one. The latter can enact "a different kind of turn" by pursuing strategies for resignifying the dominant terms of social life. We thus ultimately possess, Butler contends, the possibility of cultivating "a more open, even more ethical kind of being, one of and for the future."[36]

4.3. "Indispensable" Foundations

Let me sum up Butler's ontology as I have construed it so far. Being-in-trouble is being thrown into a "primary vulnerability to language," a dependence on "discourse we never chose." We are this "linguistic bear-

[32] *PLP*, 55, 60–62, 101.
[33] *PLP*, 62.
[34] *PLP*, 60, 64.
[35] *ES*, 125; *BTM*, 67.
[36] *PLP*, 130–31.

ing" that is always already negotiating—as we "turn"—three ontological forces: interpellating power, materialization, and the desire to desire.[37] Drawing a rough analogy with Heidegger, the *Ereignis* or "event" of being—better yet, *eventing* of being—is this turning. And, accordingly, the forces that constitute the turning function as Butler's "sources of the self." To be within their sway is to have been always already "thrown" into terms of existence that can be negotiated but not chosen. Within such an ontology, critical agency emerges not with the possibility of escaping from the turning, but rather with the possibility of continuing that turning in a somewhat different way, a way in which one redirects how the three forces continue to press upon and partially constitute one another.

With this account fleshed out, I want to turn now to the issue of its relation to the ethical-political. As I noted at the beginning of this chapter, Butler describes foundations as "indispensable." When she offers this characterization, she is speaking specifically about normative foundations for political action. She asserts that effective feminist, or gay and lesbian, politics requires affirming certain claims about identity and generalizable interests. Following Gayatri Spivak, she speaks here of an "operational essentialism" that has value only for immediate purposes, and only as long as one remembers the necessity of these normative claims being decentered at a higher level of reflection. In effect, we can never forget that such normative, foundational affirmations secure themselves only by means of a set of "exclusionary moves," through which some identities and bodies are interpellated as abject and marginal, ones that do not "matter."[38]

Of course this last claim has both ethical and ontological commitments implicit within it, as Butler is well aware. And yet this awareness is tinged with uneasiness. She expresses some reluctance toward being very explicit about this precise issue, preferring instead to assert merely that whatever justification one would be required to give here, it would not be one whose truth anchored us to some metaphysical reality, but rather one whose truth would have to be subject to the process of contestation and historical-cultural translation.[39]

This last contention is certainly one that accords with the idea of weak ontology. But there is nevertheless something in Butler's reluctance that creates a difficulty for her. I want to suggest that her aversion to too much reflection on foundations has had a negative residual effect on her own constructions. In a sense, for Butler, an effective break from strong onto-

[37] *PLP,* 2; *ES,* 26, 30.

[38] "For a Careful Reading," 133; "Contingent Foundations," 49; and "Performative Acts," 280.

[39] "For a Careful Reading," 140.

logical foundations can only be made good by articulating an austerely minimalist or thin ontology. While the imperatives of such thinness may run parallel for some distance with those of what I call weakness, the latter are not reducible to the former. Now the point of this contrast is to suggest that Butler's ontological austerity in some ways undermines the felicitousness of her project both in the sense of the adequacy of its ontological figures and in the sense of their prefiguration of ethical-political orientation.

Making good on this claim requires, first, some description of the sites where she does draw explicit, coherent connections between her ontology and ethical-political commitments. Some of the prefiguration here, as I will illustrate, is admirably done (section 4.3.A). Then I want to consider a site where a specific commitment implies an ontological figure that is, however, not articulated (section 4.3.B). Finally, I will press an argument to the effect that she is misarticulating both ontological and ethical-political reflection at another site that is crucial for any weak ontology. This concerns the conceptualization of finitude (section 4.3.C). With this issue, as well as with the preceding one of an ontological figure implied but not articulated, the root of the difficulty is traceable to Butler's tendency to ontological thinness.

4.3.A. Critical Agency and Resistance

The most carefully developed of Butler's prefigurations is one with which my overall exposition has already been entangled: critical agency and resistance. The connection between ontology and the ethical-political is here quite clear. The only problem might seem to be that the relation is the reverse of what it should be. As my unfolding of her position in section 4.2 suggested, it would be sensible to think that, for Butler, the need for ethical-political clarity actually drove the ontological construction. And this inference is probably correct. But this is not, by itself, an indication of a fault: ontology in the weak sense is never a matter of grasping being in a mode totally divorceable from ethical-political insight. A felicitous weak ontology is one where the ontology figures various existential universals that are in themselves underdetermined as to meaning, and it does so under the gravitational pull of ethical-political judgments and historical-cultural interpretations. Thus, when I speak of considering how well Butler's ontology prefigures her ethical-political orientation, it is the alignment as a whole that is crucial, not the specifics of its genesis.

Taking this slant, I find Butler's account of agency and resistance fascinating. It constitutes a real advance for Foucauldian-inspired social theory.[40] Her interpretations of language, emphasizing interpellation, reiteration, and resignification, as well as her interpretation of attachment to existence as a desire to desire that eludes full interpellation, prefigure in an original way the idea of a different turn in relation to ethical-political life, one more consciously resistant to interpellation.

One apparent weakness of this projected connection is, however, the rather vague, but recurrent, appeal to what sounds like an utterly new, "futural" ethics and politics, one that is certainly but ineffably better. Recall the statement (quoted at the end of section 4.2) to the effect that the critically turning subject is "a more open, even more ethical kind of being, one of and for the future."[41] This sort of projection is a relatively familiar one within poststructuralist and postmodern thought.[42] It carries a persistent utopian hope of a "not yet," but by itself, it remains blithely unspecific about normative orientation in the here and now. Further, the image of a utopian opening is juxtaposed with an image of modernity up to now that is reduced pretty much to unrelenting oppression. Accordingly, the grand narrative that coheres with Butler's ontology turns crucially upon the austerely simple hope for "the insurrectionary moment of . . . history, the moment that founds a future through a break with [the] past."[43]

Although the ontological figure of a different turning does indeed empower appeals to, for example, "new and future forms" of legitimation, I think this kind of inflated gesture is partially balanced in Butler's case by the insightful way she has prefigured as well an orientation to

[40] Lisa Disch has offered a very interesting example of the usefulness of Butler's approach to agency and resistance in her review essay, "Judith Butler and the Politics of the Performative," *Political Theory* 27 no. 4 (1999). Disch suggests that a full understanding of the success of Rosa Parks's now legendary act of resistance to segregation in 1955 is aided by seeing her in Butlerian terms. The fact that she could be so effective as a figure of resistance was constitutively structured by the way in which she was interpellated by the existing hierarchies of class and race. In short, she appeared as a solid, working-class woman with a middle-class demeanor: a non-trouble-making "colored" woman. As such, "she was sufficiently incongruous with the stereotypes of black criminality that were held by whites and blacks alike to challenge those stereotypes, and to precipitate a transformation of the laws that sustained them. Hers was an insurrectionary act enabled by the same racist conventions and class distinctions that it aimed to overturn. As such it is a powerful illustration of Butler's contention that although we have no choice but to oppose power from within its terms, this need not pose an impasse with respect to agency" (557).

[41] *PLP,* 131; *ES,* 90; and Judith Butler, Ernesto Laclau, and Reinaldo Laddaga, "The Uses of Equality" (an exchange), *Diacritics* 27 no. 1 (1997): 5, 10.

[42] For this criticism, see Thomas McCarthy, *Ideals and Illusions: On Reconstruction and Deconstruction in Contemporary Political Theory* (Cambridge: MIT Press, 1991), chaps. 2 and 4; and Stephen K. White, *Political Theory and Postmodernism* (New York: Cambridge University Press, 1991), 51–53, 75–84.

[43] *ES,* 158–61.

politics in the concrete present.[44] This is perhaps most clearly displayed in her thinking about a nest of questions concerning the appropriate political response to "hate speech." Here the issue is speech or images that injure or "wound" their addressees because of their race or sexuality. Now, given Butler's broadly Foucauldian lineage, her own analysis of interpellation, as well as her lesbianism, one could hardly imagine someone more sensitive to the power of "words that wound." In recent years such depth of sensitivity has often manifested itself in calls for state intervention to penalize or censor such speech. Butler, however, is highly skeptical of such calls. This skepticism is, I would suggest, engendered at least partially by her distinctive ontological perspective. My point here, as with any weak ontology, is not that the perspective determines categorically some specific political judgment, but rather that it helps engender certain dispositions toward ethical-political life that alter the affective and cognitive direction one takes into specific issues.

What disturbs Butler about calls to censor words or images that wound is the accompanying understanding they carry regarding how language, power, and subjectivity work. Language is conceived as being wielded by a power holder so as to effect the subordination of the addressee. The saying of certain words or representation of certain images performs an action, accomplishes a harm. This mode of thinking clearly draws the performative dimension of language to the fore, as Butler herself does. But there is a distinct difference here. For the prohibitionists, harmful speech is seen as having a *necessary* effect; saying necessarily does just what the speaker intends: enacting subordination and silencing the addressees in the sense of undermining their freedom to take part in public communication. Butler calls this the "illocutionary model" of hate speech. It asserts that

> hate speech constitutes its addressee at the moment of its utterance; it does not describe an injury or produce one as a consequence; it is, in the very speaking of such speech, the performance of the injury itself.[45]

Butler does not deny that there are illocutionary speech acts, but she questions whether the isolated picture of a *necessarily* effective speech act is any better as a general model of injurious speech than Althusser's isolated picture of interpellation is as a general model of the reproduction of discursive power. In both cases, too much occurs with necessity; too much sovereignty is accorded to the intentions of the speaker; and

[44] *ES*, 41.

[45] *ES*, 17–19. Butler's critique here is directed against Mari Matusuda and Catherine MacKinnon. Although the latter's argument refers to pornography, she understands this as a kind of hate speech.

too little resistant agency is accorded to the addressee. We do better to think injurious speech on a "perlocutionary" model, where saying something initiates a set of consequences or effects; this saying and its consequences are temporally distinguishable. The word and the wound do not fuse into one. The gap between them may in some cases be quite small; but its existence is crucial to emphasize, because it constitutes the space of possible failure and resignification. Butler points here to the way the word *queer* has undergone a resignification in recent years in the United States, with the addressees of hate speech in this case progressively wresting its significance away from what it has conventionally been and appropriating it as a term of pride.[46] Such an occurrence cannot even be conceptualized when one thinks in terms of the illocutionary model. Within the latter portrait, speakers wield injurious words with necessarily crushing effect; and addressees are thus automatically constituted as victims. Not only does this occlude the space of possible non-state-centered political agency, but it also perpetuates a "sovereign conceit" about actors. Those in positions of power are imagined as in full control of speech—a control limitable only by that greater sovereign, the state. And addressees are imagined as being, at least ideally, in a condition where the terms of discourse are "their own," a delusion that forgets that we are all always already interpellated in a multitude of ways.[47]

Butler's intention in critiquing the illocutionary model of hate speech is neither to minimize the injury involved nor to conclude categorically that prohibition and prosecution might not in some circumstances be defensible.[48] Rather, it is to reconfigure our initial perceptions of this whole terrain of politics and how exactly they orient us to political resistance and state power.

A second prefiguration that is quite distinctive concerns identity and identity politics. From the first articulations in *Gender Trouble,* one senses that Butler affirms an ontology that conceives being as *potentiality.* As her ontology has taken on more coherent shape, this has not changed. As she says, "we might reread being as precisely the potentiality that remains unexhausted by any particular interpellation."[49] Now this sort of formulation has the effect, as critics have noted, of making identity formations, whether individual or collective, somehow "essentially" suspect. Butler seems to be saying that we need to cultivate an attitude toward identities, according to which we "wear" them as necessary for specific purposes and "shed" them when they no longer serve those purposes. She hopes

[46] *ES,* 17, 158.
[47] *ES,* 16, 39–40.
[48] *ES,* 50, 140.
[49] *PLP,* 131.

for a political world in which "identities . . . are alternately instituted and relinquished according to the purposes at hand." Identity, Butler concludes, is best seen as nothing more than a site of "insistent rifting."[50]

I do not think that Butler's intention here is to imply, as one critic puts it, that all identity is "inherently oppressive."[51] But given her ontological formulations, it is hard to see how she can resist the slide toward this kind of implication. And if she cannot, a sense of implausibility begins to infect her entire project. I want to put this issue of identity aside for a moment and return to it after elaborating other issues of prefiguration. At that point I will explore how one might take issue with Butler on the identity question without that criticism having such damaging consequences for her project.

4.3.B. A Missing Prefiguration

As with all of the best poststructuralist and postmodern philosophy, there is in Butler a deep ethical sensibility inspiring the formulations. The conceptualizations of discourse and power are, of course, tied to a feeling for those who are constituted as "bodies that *do not* matter." This sympathy is in turn extended to some sense of the possibility of a different sort of self and community, where the stickiness of language and power would be negotiated in a more ethically admirable fashion. Butler speaks of "fundamentally more capacious, generous, and 'unthreatened' bearings of the self." Joined with this ethical image of the self is that of a political community for which the slow and careful "work of cultural translation" is central; where difference is honored in the context of an ethos that continually draws one toward the other but is alert to that interpellating insistence that always endangers the construction of interpretive schemas. In such a community, one cultivates an openness to those moments of "unexpected innocence," when the dominant terms of political discourse are brought into question by novel resignifications.[52]

The question I want to raise here is what ontological prefiguration exists for this ethos? There is the figure of a different turning, cashed out with the ideas of reiteration and the insistent desire to desire. And there is the figure of insistent interpellation. Together, these figures display a being with the difficult possibility of articulating its potential in ways not at first apparent. This way of rendering the unpredictable, irruptive quality of human action certainly provides a provocative portrait of

[50] "Force of Fantasy," 121; *GT*, 16.

[51] Fraser, "False Antitheses," 71.

[52] "For a Careful Reading," 140; *ES*, 161; "Merely Cultural," *New Left Review* 227 (January–February 1998): 38; and Butler's comment on Martha Nussbaum's essay on cosmopolitanism in *Boston Review* 14 no. 5 (1994): 18.

the existential universal of natality. What is not apparent, however, is any prefiguration of the strong sense of generosity present in Butler's ethos. By this I mean there is nothing in the ontology with which the ethical idea of *generosity toward becoming* resonates, draws sustenance.

My suspicion is that Butler would say that the only choices here are between her sort of thin ontology and a traditional, strong one, part of which might be the postulation of, say, a generous God. Only something of the latter sort could provide an ontological prefiguration for a generous ethos. Given that choice, Butler could feel content with her option. But the choices are, I think, more numerous. Taylor, for example, represents the possibility of a *weak* ontology with a God. And might there not be a way of figuring something like generosity within a nontheistic, weak ontology? This would be the sort of option against which one might appropriately criticize Butler for a failure of ontological richness.

Let me draw here again on the later Heidegger's notion of *Ereignis,* the eventing or presencing of being, as well as his notion of *Gestell,* that disposition toward being which he finds to be so prevalent in the modern West. *Gestell* refers to a disposition within which being is taken as stuff to be grasped, mastered, and used by a disengaged subject. The shift Heidegger wants to encourage is one in which there is a relaxation of this posture of grasping. One cultivates an attitude more receptive to the sheer "event" of the presencing or "worlding" of being: its continual becoming in a profuse, unmanageable manifold. What I am particularly concerned to highlight in this ontology is the connotation of *giving* that is implied when Heidegger continually speaks here of the *Es gibt* of being. This familiar, everyday German phrase is typically translated as "there is" or "there are," as in "There is a tree in the park." But the verb in this phrase is *geben,* "to give." And it is to this aspect of the phrase that Heidegger wants to draw attention. The presencing of being, its manifolding, is a "giving" to us.[53]

My point in this sketch of relatively familiar Heideggerian concepts is intended simply to suggest one way in which a kind of generosity might be figured in an ontology that does not include, as necessary, a God.[54] Of course, such a figure, by itself, does not automatically prefigure a notion of ethical generosity such as the one Butler affirms. Indeed, Heidegger's own work bears sad testimony to the possibility of such a gap.

[53] Heidegger, "Zeit und Sein," in *Zur Sache des Denkens* (Tübingen: Max Niemayer, 1969), 5 ff. None of what I have just said should be interpreted as claiming that *the* character of being is reflected in language. My point is simply that linguistic expressions can suggest to us unfamiliar ways in which to figure being.

[54] The issue of what sort of theism is in Heidegger's later work can, it seems to me, be held aside here. The coherence and attractiveness of this notion of the "giving" of being can be appreciated without the necessity of its being backed by a God.

What this ontological figure of "giving" does do, however, is allow one to throw into relief the character of Butler's world. It is a world of pressures, demands, insistences, a world in which one is hard pressed to see any ontological prefiguration of that virtue of generosity upon which her ethical-political hopes so crucially turn. But it is only with the cultivation of such a virtue that Butler's moments of "unexpected innocence" will occur at all.

4.3.C. Vivifying Finitude

I want to turn now to a problem in Butler that has to do not with the lack of ontological prefiguration of an explicit ethical affirmation, but with a site where both the ontological figure and the ethical sensibility seem misarticulated. In order to get a sense of the significance of this issue, let me return to an issue laid aside earlier, namely Butler's view that identity is best interpreted as nothing more than a site of "insistent rifting."[55]

She is brought to this extreme formulation because anything short of it seems to her to imply necessarily aligning identity with some sort of ontologically secured essence or "home," which in turn functions only to mask power and convention. Her central notion of human being as sheer potentiality straining against the adhesiveness of interpellation is intended to prefigure just such a decentered place for identity in ethics and politics. "Proliferation," struggling free of given terms of identity, is a value that trumps any other.[56] One is, of course, never free of identity formations—of terms not one's own—but one can learn to bear them lightly, shed them more readily.

As I said earlier, it is difficult not to sympathize here with critics who find that Butler's ontology prefigures an ethical-political world in which all identity is somehow oppressive. In short, she has no ontological figure that lends the stickiness or adhesiveness of identity anything other than a negative value. This lack ultimately has something to do, I think, with the problem of providing a satisfactory ontological rendering of finitude.

Human being, for Butler, is becoming, potentiality, proliferation, the movement of desire to desire. Curiously, the fact that this becoming *ceases* at some point for me and her is of no constitutive concern. In this forgetting, Butler makes us into, as it were, proliferation creatures of infinite duration. We reiterate without end. For creatures such as this, identity categories are at best grist for further proliferation.

[55] "Force of Fantasy," 121.
[56] *GT*, x, 93.

In one way, Butler does attend quite specifically to the fear of death, at least in the sense of "social death." Her discussion of the depth of our passionate attachment to the terms of "linguistic survival" is quite provocative, as is her insight that real challenges to dominant social norms may require a willingness to risk a kind of linguistic death.[57] Such a line of thought might provide an interesting defense against Taylor's critique that Nietzsche's (and Foucault's) progeny are drawn invariably toward the dangerous idea of making death a "work."[58]

Butler would indeed have us make our own "social death" a work, but that would not seem necessarily to imply the kind of violence about which Taylor worries.

Although symbolic death may be related to death in many ways, the two are nevertheless obviously not the same; and Butler's ontology figures the latter as something of surprisingly minor concern.[59] She would have us cultivate a deep sense of being always in a condition of "prior linguistic vulnerability" to terms not our own, but sees no necessity for thematizing our mortality as that which confronts us in a different way with terms not our own.

Butler mentions life and death in her discussion of the "array of 'materialities' that pertain to the body, that which is signified by the domains of biology, anatomy, physiology, hormonal and chemical composition, illness, age, weight, metabolism, life and death." These "materialities" constitute a "persistent" force on human consciousness, but they are not fully identifiable, ontologically, prior to the variable "interpretive matrices" through which we always encounter them.[60] In general, there is nothing implausible about this strong hermeneutical way of proceeding here. What is questionable, however, is how "life and death" are simply arrayed in a list of phenomenal "domains" like our "chemical composition" or "weight." In weak ontological terms, she has failed to give any distinctive figuration to the existential universal of finitude. What she needs is some rendering comparable to the one she gives language, when she comprehends human being as constituted through "a linguistic bearing" toward one another: a "structure of address as both linguistic vulnerability and exercise." The relation of such "linguistic bearing" to human beings is that it is "something without which they *could not be said to exist.*"[61] My

[57] *PLP,* 28–29; *ES,* 132–36.

[58] See section 3.2.B.

[59] *ES,* 133–36. My point here is not that death is of no concern to Butler. She has written movingly about AIDS in general (more on that later) and about the death of a friend; see her introduction to Linda Singer, *Erotic Welfare: Sexual Theory and Politics in the Age of Epidemic,* ed. J. Butler and M. MacGrogan (New York: Routledge, 1993), 1–15. My point concerns specifically the ontological figuration of mortality.

[60] *BTM,* 66–67.

[61] *ES,* 30; my emphasis.

point here is simply that a felicitous weak ontology owes us, for comparable reasons, a comparable figuration of the structure of finitude.

A constitutive part of the stickiness of human beings is being stuck on a journey we never chose; we did not select its starting place and we cannot change the kind of end it will have. This end confronts us necessarily with a gap between the human and the beyond human. Finitude is, to speak like Butler, a distinctive "that which" which demands our interpretive efforts. Were Butler to have given finitude more ontological force in her account, then it would have been less easy for her to reduce identity merely to the status of a site for ceaseless rifting. For her, identity formations are clothes to be shed according to the purposes at hand. But if we think of the structure of finitude as a journey of limited duration, then the clothes we wear are not simply a subset of all potential attire. The crux of things here is not that all identity formations remain fixed, but rather that even the new ones I struggle into become part of that set of the only ones I will ever wear.[62] Identity, in its particularity, has, accordingly, a kind of weight for human being that is poorly comprehended when understood only as oppressive. Butler's mistake here is curiously analogous to that of some orthodox liberals who find arguments about the weight of culture to be of marginal significance, because, it is asserted, the "freewheeling," disengaged self can live "in a kaleidoscope of cultures." The changing of one's culture, even when it is not a particularly free choice, is thus to be taken as a relatively costless shift.[63]

An instructive way to highlight the significance of the insight about the weight of identity (whether sexual, familial, cultural, etc.) is to bring it to bear upon Butler's own sense of what the ethos of a good political community should be. She emphasizes, as shown above, the central importance of the difficult and careful work of "cultural translation" across differences of identity. The crucial question to pose here is this: How careful will I really be in interpretive encounters, if at heart I take the other's particular identity formations to be just so much congealed potentiality that needs to be loosened up? In a certain sense, I just won't see the point of carefulness in my engagement with the other's identity.[64]

[62] Cf. the related concern of Kathleen Jones, *Compassionate Authority*, 218.

[63] The statement about living "in a kaleidoscope of cultures" is from Jeremy Waldron. He is quoted and criticized by Will Kymlicka, *Multicultural Citizenship: A Liberal Theory of Minority Right* (Oxford: Oxford University Press, 1995), 84–85. See Waldron, "Minority Cultures and the Cosmopolitan Alternative," *University of Michigan Journal of Law Reform* 25 no. 3 (1992).

[64] "For a Careful Reading," 140. One might compare Butler's problem here with a difficulty I noted in Kateb's Emersonian reading of "soul." The specific formulations are quite different, but each subtly encourages a certain carelessness. In Kateb's case, since my "soul" contains all human possibilities, in some sense I always already know the other as well as she

Understanding identity in relation to a vivified sense of finitude can, however, provide just such a point. And yet it does not have to accomplish this at the cost of according that weight the significance of truth; in short, one is not according it the status of one's true essence, one's secure home in a particular identity. For a nontheistic, weak ontology, such a seeking of final security is precisely a forgetting of finitude. The pleasures of this kind of homecoming induce an inattentiveness to the constitutive gap between the human and the beyond human. Vivifying finitude in everyday life means cultivating a quiet, ongoing resistance to finding one's truth in some identity; but it also means giving place to the constitutive weight of concrete identity.

4.4. The Insistent Ambivalence of Loss

Up to this point, I have characterized Butler's ontology as comprised of three modes of insistence; and I have criticized it to a degree for its tendency to thinness. Now I want to allow this picture to become somewhat thicker by turning to a topic whose ontological implications will perhaps be more readily apparent when it is taken up against the background of my preceding discussion.

In *The Psychic Life of Power* (1997), Butler engages the issue of melancholia. This is part of her broader exploration of how Foucauldian social theory should understand psychic life. In what follows, I first want to elucidate Butler's notion of melancholia with an eye to drawing out its ontological dimensions (section 4.4.A). Then I consider what difference this makes in relation to the enrichment of her overall ontology, both in terms of its prefiguration of ethical-political insight and its figuration of finitude (section 4.4.B).

4.4.A. Melancholia

In a 1917 essay, Freud developed an account of the psychological condition of "melancholia" through a contrast with "mourning" *(Trauer)*.[65] Both, he explained, were reactions to the trauma of the loss of an object of love or desire. Mourning is, in short, the healthy resolution of this situation; the person comes to accept the loss and go on with his/her life. Melancholia, on the contrary, is Freud's description of a syndrome

---

does herself. Her voice becomes curiously secondary. In Butler's case, that voice, insofar as it adheres to a particular identity formation, falls categorically under the judgment of a "symptomatic reading."

[65] Sigmund Freud, "Mourning and Melancholia," in *General Psychological Theory: Papers on Metapsychology*, ed. P. Rieff (New York: Collier, 1963), 164–79.

of symptoms associated with a failure to accept the loss. Instead of giving up the object, the person internalizes it in such a way that the ego becomes a substitute for that object. And yet, since the ego is ultimately an unsatisfying substitute, it becomes not just the site of love but also hate and aggression. Above all, it is this "ambivalence that distinguishes melancholia."[66]

Butler pushes Freud's reflections in a number of distinctive directions. First, the trajectory of desire that is melancholia is not fully explainable, she contends, as one possible scenario within the preexisting internal psychic space of ego and superego. Rather we must carry the issue of loss and our reaction to it into speculation about the very constitution of this psychic topography in early childhood. She wants to suggest that early "object" losses—of the mother as an object of desire and of the same sex as an object of desire—which are crucial to the constitution of the ego are always already entangled with the ambivalent reactions of melancholia. Butler sums up this line of reflection with the assertion that "there can be no ego without melancholia." Moreover, if melancholia plays such a role, then it is not something like an unhealthy variant of mourning, but rather something that "makes mourning possible."[67]

Accordingly, melancholia takes on a peculiar status: "Melancholia does not name a psychic process that might be recounted through an adequate [psychoanalytic] explanatory scheme." Instead, it "returns us to the figure of the 'turn' as a founding trope." In effect, rather than a psycho-logic that describes the possible economy of certain psychic entities, Butler is offering further elaboration of her onto-logic. It is, I think, best described as another dimension of that onto-logic of turning that I have already explicated. The "melancholic turn" refers specifically to the *re*direction of attachment from the object to that which is constituted by this redirected force of desire: "the psychic topography of super-ego/ego" that is traversed by ambivalence. The significance of Butler's emphasis on this turn is that it installs an "ambivalent reaction to loss" as a constituent of human being in a way that is not reducible to analysis in terms of any of the other three ontological insistences that I distinguished earlier.[68] In short, with this notion of the force of loss and the ambivalence it necessarily engenders, Butler delineates a fourth mode of constitutive insistence.

Although the ambivalence of loss is a distinctive insistence, its manifestation is always intertwined with the other three. Obviously that which

[66] *PLP,* 168–69, 171, 187.

[67] *PLP,* 170–71, 174, 178. Butler suggests that Freud himself later came to just this conclusion.

[68] *PLP,* 168, 174.

one loses may be intimately related to that which one acquires through the attachments engendered by interpellation. This connection is brought out clearly in the instance of melancholia to which Butler directs the most attention: "gender melancholy." In her interpretation, the interpellated "accomplishment of heterosexual 'being' " takes place through a primary "foreclosure of homosexuality" in early childhood: the loss of the possibility of the same sex as an object of desire. But this loss, constitutive yet disavowed, has a continuing effect, because it marks "the limit to the subject's sense of *pouvoir,* its sense of what it can accomplish and, in that sense, its power." The subjectivity that is constituted by interpellation is thus also "haunted by an inassimilable remainder," which emerges as gender melancholy.[69]

A heterosexual society is thus characterized by a "constitutive melancholy." As a result, the homosexual signifies for the heterosexual "an object which, if loved, would spell destruction." This pervasive threat of dissolution of self, when combined with the aggressiveness spawned by the melancholic reaction, creates a potent mix in terms of social power. For the aggressiveness that is initially self-directed in the symptoms of heightened self-beratement of conscience can be turned outward as well. The interpellative power of naming is thereby redoubled in force, for it can effectively enact a political "delineation of the field of . . . objects . . . marked for death."[70]

Melancholia thus appears to signify another sort of deep vulnerability to power. But just as with the stubborn attachment portrayed earlier, here as well there is some possibility of beginning to turn slightly, but significantly, differently. Just as the detachability of desire gives us the possibility of critical subjectivity in general, so in this dimension it opens the possibility of working melancholy into mourning. Given the constitutive character Butler assigns to loss and ambivalence, this possibility is not to be imagined as the total transcendence of the effects of melancholy, either by the individual or society. Accordingly, what Butler means here is merely the idea of turning, working, cultivating oneself in a different direction. With regard to the problem of gender melancholy, this would mean, for example, contesting public discourse that marks gays and lesbians as objects that are in essence ungrievable and whose deaths from AIDS are thus in some sense relatively acceptable to the dominant heterosexual population. Avowing loss here would mean taking seriously "the task of finding a public occasion and language in which to grieve this seemingly endless number of deaths."[71]

[69] *PLP,* 23, 29, 162.

[70] *PLP,* 23, 27. Butler also analyzes the issue of "gay melancholy," 147–50.

[71] *PLP,* 138.

4.4.B. Constitutive Loss

Let's consider more closely the underlying claims that animate this line of thought. Butler's assertions are quite strong. In the case of sexuality, the constitutive loss of the same sex as an object of desire manifests itself in the dominant heterosexual population as a "pervasive melancholy." Butler would even suggest that ours is "a culture of gender melancholy," exhibiting both aggression toward gays and lesbians and an incapacity to grieve the immense loss of life from AIDS.[72]

This sort of wholesale projection of individual pathology onto the level of cultural character always tends to raise as many questions as it answers. For example, one might ask here: Does Butler's claim really extend equally to all heterosexual societies throughout history and across cultures? Although such questions are amply warranted here, pushing them too hard, however, would miss a key point. Butler freely admits that her claims about melancholy are somewhat "hyperbolic." In this sense, her characterization of a melancholic society is intended to have an effect analogous to Foucault's characterization of a "disciplinary" one; that is, its primary intention is to jolt us in specific ways and reorient our attention. In this case the jolt is to involve how we think about gender and political life, more specifically the patterns according to which identity, sexual desire, repudiation, and aggression circulate. Understood in this fashion, Butler's assertions about our melancholic society sound less implausible. The analysis of melancholy is not presenting itself as the psychoanalytic, explanatory truth of our culture, but rather as providing some of the terms of a "dramatic language" for attending very differently to undeniably significant political problems.[73]

It is important at this point not to let this hyperbolic gesture in regard to gender melancholy engulf the entire sense of Butler's claims about loss and ambivalence. She is thematizing a constitutive insistence of human being that is not limited in scope to issues of sexuality. Seen in this light, one finds the reflections on ambivalence and loss starting to come into focus as precisely the sort of figuration of finitude that I have argued was lacking earlier.[74]

My complaint about finitude was couched in terms of Butler's reading of identity as a kind of infinite potentiality, definable merely as a site of "insistent rifting." The rifting occurs, of course, on the terms initially set by interpellation, but those terms are open to what is effectively infinite

[72] *PLP,* 138, 140.

[73] *PLP,* 149–150.

[74] Although Butler mentions melancholia in *BTM* (111–13, 242), her views on it are not distinctively articulated until *PLP.*

resignification. The new emphasis, however, gives this site an additional stickiness. Loss and the ambivalence it entails are not aspects of identity one can simply shed. They set parameters for who I can be and what shape my identity can take. "There is no break with the *constitutive historicity of loss* to which melancholy attests."[75] With this shift in her thinking, then, Butler provides that specific weight or density for identity that had been missing, and whose lack has helped encourage the criticism that all identity is, in her eyes, "oppressive."

Identity, in this new formulation, is no more inherently "oppressive" than gravity. As a result, this means that Butler's ontology will not prefigure a radicalism that is incapable of distinguishing between this constitutive density of identity and further, more questionable, claims about truth in identity. This point is crucial in how one engages the "other" ethically and politically. Without a figuration of this density, an ethos of generosity will tend to slip subtly and too quickly into frustration, impatience, and a preemptively strategic attitude.

The connection between melancholy and mourning also plays a crucial role in the more adequate figuration of finitude. When loss and ambivalence are constitutive of human being in the way Butler suggests, then the idea of a different turning becomes intrinsically intertwined both with continually working on aggression and mourning loss.

Mourning now gains a sense that is not restricted to an attitude taken up on the occasion of a specific loss. It can become a more complex, persisting disposition, within which one attends more consciously to the kind of being one is. Loss just is constitutive of us; and our ethos of everyday life can be infused with a disposition that attends to that reality or with ones that ignore it. The disengaged self is an entity that lives in such blissful ignorance. It is autonomous, sovereign, always in a sense almost infinite in its possibilities. It is "a subject who might already be something without its losses." But if loss and its trace are always constitutive, then to accept such a picture of "autonomy . . . is to forget that trace." The specific sense that mourning takes on within this ontological figuration is of a remembering, an avowal of loss, of "unlived possibility."[76] This avowal becomes then a central way in which a being for whom loss is constitutive disposes itself to its finitude.

By itself, such an approach to mourning might seem to prefigure an ethos of overly passive humility. But here one sees the value of engaging the topic of finitude initially through melancholia. When the issue is not only one of loss, but also ambivalence, there remains the question of

[75] *PLP,* 194. Cf. Adam Phillips, whose comments are included in *PLP:* "Keep It Moving: Commentary on Judith Butler's 'Melancholy Gender/Refused Identification,' " 156.

[76] *PLP,* 139, 195–96.

aggression. Turning differently thus must involve not only mourning but also a sort of work on the aggression and resentment entailed by loss. This counteraggressiveness can be exerted in two alternative, related directions. First, it can be turned upon the excessive self-beratements of conscience; that is, against conscience that is "heightened" by an aggressive moral rigorism. And, secondly, it can be turned upon political life insofar as it enlists such rigorism in its marking out of some social subjects as officially ungrievable or "marked for death."[77]

Thus, the ontological thematization of ambivalent loss gives Butler a way of prefiguring an activist, contestatory ethos of self-artistry and political commitment. Within such a world, a recourse to passive humility alone fails to engage adequately the terms of one's human predicament. Simple humility, in hoping to finesse aggressiveness, will always run the danger of quietly intensifying its righteousness with an unconsciously accumulating reservoir of aggressiveness. The notion of the "melancholic turn" of human being thus also preserves in a modified form the Nietzchean warning about some of the implicit dangers in Christianity. In doing so, I think Butler provides an interesting challenge to a theistic weak ontology such as Taylor's. Despite his acceptance of the burden of guilt that Christianity bears for its history of violence, has he probed adequately the dynamics of conscience, humility, and aggressiveness?

The portrait that I have drawn in this chapter of Butler as a weak ontologist is one that, at points, may seem forced in its characterization. Clearly her negative gestures against modes of strong ontology are more explicitly elaborated than the affirmative shaping of something different. But, as I have tried to show, there is ample evidence of the growing presence of the latter activity in Butler's work. And when this activity is assessed against the standards I elaborated for a felicitous weak ontology, Butler actually comes off reasonably well, especially in her most recent work, where she has untangled some knots tied earlier. My strong reading is, in effect, a challenge to her to continue in this direction, but in an even more self-conscious way. This would mean acknowledging more clearly that she has been thickening her ontology to such a degree that her implicit sense of it as "thin"—and thus in need of little discussion—is now no longer plausible.

Were she to do this and accept the model of weak ontology as appropriate, she would then need to attend more to a variety of further issues that this model pushes to the fore. First of all, she would need to affirm consistently that her notion of "turning" is not simply a linguistic trope, but rather also an ontological figuration that portrays human presencing

[77] *PLP*, 183–94.

as the articulation of the four insistences she delineates.[78] These function, I would suggest, as Butler's sources of the self. If she were to embrace this interpretation, she would then, in turn, need to become more lucid in her account of their collective sense. In surveying the course of her work, one gets the feeling that she has worked her way toward the significance of each of these four insistences in different contexts and has not yet devoted adequate reflection to what the four, taken together, finally constitute as a thinking of human being. Another pressing question, as I tried to show earlier, concerns how well her strong ethical affirmation of generosity and "new and future forms" of legitimation cohere with her ontological figures.[79]

The kind of deficits Butler has should become clearer in the course of the next chapter. Like Butler, Connolly wants to delineate a self and its sources that resists "the imagination of wholeness"; that is, the conjuring up of "terms which really are one's own."[80] But Connolly goes a good deal farther in elucidating the sense of a self that resists this imagining, as well as the sources that might animate such resistance. Since Connolly does elaborate his ontology more fully and consciously, I want to wait until the next chapter to consider more extensively how well a representative of weak ontology in the Nietzchean-Foucauldian tradition can meet the challenge that Taylor issues in regard to its claimed affinity for violence.

A further important issue for Butler emerges in her recent treatment of melancholy. One of my main claims has been that the thematization of melancholy allowed Butler to provide a figuration of finitude, which in turn chastened what would otherwise be an image of human being as an infinite-becoming-machine. But this salutary shift also makes starker the apparent absence of another kind of chastening with which a weak ontology must be concerned. There should be some point at which the ontology folds back upon itself, in the sense of chastening the momentum of its claim to have grasped being correctly. I suspect that Butler's relative neglect of this question reflects an at least implicit sense that a *thin* ontology has already adequately admitted its contestability. The idea would be that the thinner the ontological figures, the less one has to worry about contestability. There may be some truth in this idea, but unless one thins down to nothing, the issue of signaling the limits of one's ontology remains to some degree.

[78] *PLP*, 3–4.

[79] *ES*, 41.

[80] *Why I Am Not a Secularist* (Minneapolis: University of Minnesota Press, 1999), 143 ff.

Although Butler does not confront this issue extensively, she nevertheless touches upon it and in a fashion that may begin to fold her ontology back upon itself. One of the central claims of her perspective is, of course, that sexual difference is a performative *accomplishment,* not a natural *disposition.* And yet, in her discussion of melancholy, she admits that sexual difference "in some cases . . . is *both*" accomplishment and disposition.[81] If I am reading her correctly here, she is indicating an awareness that her ontology does not have to assert its seamless fit with reality in order to be persuasive. Some fit, sure; but a comparable degree of fit may also be available to other ontologies. Although she thus cannot deliver a knockout punch to dispositional ontologies on truth grounds, Butler—in good, weak-ontological style—shifts the contest to aesthetic-affective and ethical terrain. Here she appeals simply to how her approach employs a "dramatic language" within which we can think ourselves as "more mobile" in our identity than we would otherwise be.[82]

With these last points about sources of the self, prefiguration, and folds, I mean only to suggest some further places at which Butler's project could be brought into more constructive engagement with the standards of weak ontology. The larger, background issue is whether Butler is willing to become more explicit about, and more comfortable with, this entire activity of ontology in a different voice.

[81] *PLP,* 165–66; my emphasis.
[82] *PLP,* 150, 166.

Chapter Five

THE ONTOLOGY AND POLITICS OF A "POST-NIETZSCHEAN SENSIBILITY": WILLIAM CONNOLLY

LIKE TAYLOR, William Connolly is quite explicit about the importance of attending to the "ontological dimension of political thought." As he says, "every interpretation presupposes or invokes some . . . problematical stance with respect to the fundamental character of being."[1] And, of course, the qualifier "problematical" indicates that Connolly is not pursuing a project with strong ontological characteristics. The variant of ontology that he elaborates draws sustenance, like Butler's, from the work of Nietzsche and Foucault. But unlike any of these thinkers, Connolly has methodically enacted an affirmative turn. By this I mean he has engaged extensively the question: Within what modes of affirmation—ontological, ethical, and political—should we locate the critical insights and techniques of genealogy? Connolly remains a strong believer in the value of genealogy for decentering and detaching us from conventional dispositions and presumptions, but he argues that adherents to this mode of critique must realize that

> detachment from any particular set of dispositions and presumptions inevitably attaches me to another set. It is hard, indeed impossible, to become detached as such. So it is important to articulate the ideal to which your strategies of critical detachment are attaching you.[2]

Fully articulating such an affirmative "ideal" involves elaborating ontological claims, sketching a congruent "ethical sensibility," and using those insights for a "rethinking of democratic theory." In my terms, Connolly is advancing on all the fronts that I have identified as necessary

The following abbreviations will be used for referring to Connolly's books.

AI — *The Augustinian Imperative: A Reflection on the Politics of Morality.* Newbury Park, Calif.: Sage Publications, 1993.

EP — *The Ethos of Pluralization.* Minneapolis: University of Minnesota Press, 1995.

ID — *Identity/Difference: Democratic Negotiations of Political Paradox.* Ithaca, N.Y.: Cornell University, Press, 1991.

WNS — *Why I Am Not a Secularist.* Minneapolis: University of Minnesota Press, 1999.

[1] *EP,* xxv, 1; *AI,* 149.

[2] *EP,* 35

today for a felicitous, weak ontological "foundation" in political theory. The scope and specific direction of his efforts are succinctly expressed in the statement that he "seeks to translate the late-modern experience of the rich *an-arche* of being into enactment of a more generous pluralism."[3]

In section 5.1, I take up the particular ontological figures Connolly develops and ask whether his understanding of ontology is compatible with my notion of weak ontology. In addition, I consider the particularly provocative fashion in which Connolly highlights the significance of sensibility and cultivation for ethical-political affirmation.

In section 5.2, I examine the kind of "ethos of democracy" that is prefigured by Connolly's ontology.[4] How exactly are we to understand the "translation" of ontological figures into a more "generous" form of political pluralism? And what are the specific qualities of this revised pluralism? Like Taylor, Connolly directly confronts some of the basic components of liberalism. In particular, he argues, first, that the idea of justice defended by political liberals is deficient unless it is relativized to the "more fundamental" idea of "critical responsiveness." In the process of weighing this claim, I will also turn back to consider Taylor's charge that there is an ineluctable fascination with death and violence in an ontology like Connolly's that affirms an "external, amoral source."

A second confrontation with political liberalism emerges from Connolly's claim that the "historical modus vivendi of secularism," with which the liberal idea of the public sphere is entangled, "is coming apart at the seams." Accordingly, a refashioned notion of political discourse is needed in which we engage more directly the deep divergences between the ontological sources honored today by different constituencies. This new sense of *what* should be brought into political discourse is complemented by a different sense of *how* one engages in political contest.[5]

5.1. Figuring and Cultivating Being as Rich and Fugitive

At the core of Connolly's reflections on self, other, and world is a bold figuration of the richness or abundance of being (section 5.1.A). After elucidating this figure, I turn to consider whether his characterization of this project as an "ont*a*logy" makes it compatible with my notion of weak ontology (section 5.1.B). Finally, I examine how Connolly emphasizes issues of sensibility and cultivation (section 5.1.C). Of the thinkers considered in this book, none expends greater effort upon the aesthetic-affective dimension than Connolly; more specifically upon the necessity

[3] *AI*, 140; *EP*, 28.
[4] *AI*, 152.
[5] *EP*, xv, 187; *WNS*, 19–20.

of cultivating a sensibility that is congruent with one's basic ontological figures. Aesthetic-affective work on the self is also crucial to how one engages others ethically and politically. This insight is present as well in Kateb, Taylor, and Butler, but Connolly entangles it with the question of ontological contestability in a distinctive fashion. As I said in chapter 1, a felicitous weak ontology does not simply declare its contestability, but rather enacts it in some way, in the sense of turning the unifying momentum of its concepts back upon itself. One of the fascinating things about Connolly in this respect is how elaborately his notion of the cultivation of an ethical sensibility weaves the force of contestability into the fabric of everyday practice.

5.1.A. Unmanageable and without Purpose

The familiar image of the disengaged self implies an agent whose identity is secure; in fact, that security is what allows one the confidence to envision life as a self-controlled project in which one powers oneself through the world. The need to maintain such a sense of confidence encourages this self to shuffle certain sorts of discordant experiences quickly out of consciousness. These are experiences that strike us with "the contingency of life and the fragility of things," that threaten us in our very "home." Connolly calls this the experience of the "uncanny."[6] It includes mundane moments of temporary cognitive disorientation, bodily unruliness such as when one's heart pounds uncontrollably in moments of nervousness, as well as massive shocks like the sudden loss of a loved one. Each such event recalls to us, lightly or powerfully, the limits of our power to form and control, of our ability to project ourselves confidently in the world and hold others in reasonably fixed orbits around us. Uncanniness tends to elicit feelings of anxiety.

For Connolly, the crucial issue is how we choose to work on such feelings. For one invested in a self-image of disengagement, anxiety is heightened because the uncanny threatens the sense of distance necessary to sustain expectations of potential control and secure identity. Anxiety here can easily blend into resentment and a desire for revenge, if one can identify some agents who seem responsible for such disturbances. Alternatively, we might ascribe the uncanny to a transcendent source, a god whose will allows one to sort out the significance of such experience in terms of an intrinsic moral order. Connolly, however, is interested in ways of cultivating the experience of the uncanny that generate a momentum of thought and feeling that runs counter to these two familiar

[6] *ID,* 25; *AI,* xx, 3, 9–12. Connolly draws here from Freud's idea of the *Unheimlich,* but gives it an extended meaning; see *AI,* 132–38.

alternatives, which in different ways imply a fixity of being. If we figure being differently, we may no longer experience the uncanny as simply unwanted disruption or as testimony to be aligned within a secure theological matrix of good and evil. The underlying problem with these alternatives is that each

> demands that the world, be *for us* in the last instance, either as a dispenser of rewards for virtue or as a pliable medium susceptible to human mastery. . . . Both demand compensation, either from a god who installs providence into nature or from a plastic world that has lost this god.[7]

Ultimately, for Connolly, there is something narcissistic about this demand that the world *be for us.* He affirms instead "a protean vitality of being": the world is neither simply a container of "plastic matter to be used" nor the manifestation of "intrinsic purpose," but rather an ultimately unmanageable presencing of "diverse energies and strange vitalities." If we begin to think-feel the world in this way, we may also begin to take the "fugitive difference" that constitutes the uncanny not as something necessarily in need of mastery or moral categorization, but rather as something to be prized as a manifestation of the "abundance" or "richness of being."[8]

Connolly finds this idea in Nietzsche; or rather, as he admits, in "my Nietzsche," a phrase indicating an intention to emphasize some of that philosopher's insights and dissent from or ignore others.[9] My attention will not be focused on the specifics of Connolly's choices in this regard, but rather on the overall coherence of the "post-Nietzschean" ontology he crafts.

Whatever the precise source of this rendering of protean, unmanageable excess *as* richness or abundance, it is helpful to turn again to Heidegger's notion of the "eventing" of being as an *anonymous giving.* The sense of *Es gibt,* or "it gives," with the *it* being as anonymous as the *it* of *it is raining,* helps highlight a crucial shift of ontological frame that is occurring, within which the appropriate orientation of human being becomes one of gratitude. This is a distinctive kind of gratitude, however, because its expression has no giving agent as its object. You are not grateful *to* a subject, in this case God.[10]

The juxtaposition with Heidegger is useful here not only for the similarity that it highlights but also for the deep differences that come into focus. For the later Heidegger, the eventing of being is in a curious way

[7] *AI,* 9–11.

[8] *AI,* 9–10, 136–37; *ID,* 120; *EP,* 16–19; *WNS,* 54.

[9] *WNS,* 52–54.

[10] Cf. *AI,* 144–45 n. 11.

something that takes place outside of the self and beyond the dynamics of self and other. Heidegger's main worry is that, in our current existential forgetfulness, we fail to comprehend the authentic character of being. We need to release ourselves from a techno-"enframing" of the world *(Gestell)* to an attitude of "letting be" *(Gelassenheit)* as the appropriate way to show gratitude.[11] This is a shift in how we come at the world, as well as in how we allow it to come at us. Now clearly this shift involves cultivating a change in the self. But, for Connolly, such an understanding of work on the self is radically incomplete; it abstracts too much from the corporeal, "visceral register of being," and it neglects entirely ethical-political dynamics of self and other. When these dimensions are taken into account, work on the self involves a variety of new sorts of complex activities.[12]

Connolly adds the element of the visceral when he says that we experience the unmanageable presencing or becoming of the world as both "internal energies and external forces." They flow over and through us in ways that belie attempts to portray the self as essentially disengaged either instrumentally or noumenally. Images of ourselves as sovereign, calculating egos or pure Kantian wills, bringing the world into line instrumentally or morally, require too much suppression of what we cannot help experiencing. In regard to "internal energies," Connolly draws on recent neurophysiological research on the brain to support his point. This work shows images of disengagement to be based, explicitly or implicitly, on outdated notions of a single, unified center of reason and will, whereas in reality there are multiple "brains," including the amygdala and a "simple cortical complex" in the breast, that register messages in ways that generate intense feelings of fear, disgust, anxiety, and joy before conscious, rational processing takes place.

> Moreover these visceral modes of appraisal are often very intense, carrying considerable energy and fervancy with them into the other registers of being. This "invisible" set of intensive appraisals forms (as I will call it) an infrasensible subtext from which conscious thoughts, feelings and discursive judgments draw part of their sustenance.[13]

Connolly speaks of these visceral appraisals as being constituted from "thought-imbued intensities," a term he uses to emphasize the intermingling of a bodily, affective aspect and a cognitive, cultural aspect. This is

[11] See my discussion in *Political Theory and Postmodernism* (Cambridge: Cambridge University Press, 1991), chaps. 3 and 4.

[12] *WNS,* 3, 29.

[13] *WNS,* 27–29, 175–76; "Techniques of Thought and Practices of Ethics," manuscript, 1998, 2–6.

because our reactions of, say, immediate disgust may be both corporeal and yet culturally variable. Interestingly, Connolly suggests that we might think of this immanent field of thought-imbued intensities as a "contending interpretation" of Kant's transcendental field, since it both operates partially outside of the direct reach of consciousness and is effective in influencing both conduct and thought. When we think in these terms, we are less likely to be captured by images of the self as disengaged, sovereign calculator or as implementing the dictates of pure practical reason; and we are more likely to think about ethics as an activity that includes a central place for the idea of cultivation in the sense of "modest" work on these culturally imbued intensities and their influence on our perceptions and judgments.[14]

Connolly's emphasis on the visceral presencing of being is complemented by his attention to a distinctive intersubjective dynamic of presencing. For the later Heidegger, there are only individual selves, each faced with the work of shedding the ontological attitude of *Gestell.* For Connolly, that picture ignores the specific becoming of human identity.

Drawing upon themes in both Nietzsche and Foucault, Connolly expresses this becoming as follows:

> My identity is what I am and how I am recognized rather than what I choose, want, or consent to. It is the dense self from which choosing, wanting, and consenting proceed. Without that density, these acts could not occur; with it, they are recognized to be mine. *Our* identity, in a similar way, is what we are and the basis from which we proceed.
>
> An identity is established in relation to a series of differences that have become socially recognized. These differences are essential to its being. If they did not coexist as differences, it would not exist in its distinctness and solidity. Entrenched in this indispensable relationship is a second set of tendencies, themselves in need of exploration, to congeal established identities into fixed forms, thought and lived as if their structure expressed the true order of things. When these pressures prevail, the maintenance of one identity (or field of identities) involves the conversion of some differences into otherness, into evil, or one of its numerous surrogates. Identity requires difference in order to be, and it converts difference into otherness in order to secure its own self-certainty.[15]

The becoming of human being is the constituting of identity through difference. Difference forms the constitutive background against which identity struggles to appearance. This much is onto-logic. But Connolly speaks as well in the passage above of "tendencies" that adhere to this

[14] *WNS,* 27–28; "Techniques of Thought," 7.

[15] *ID,* 164.

onto-logic. These tendencies refer to the human temptations to take what is an accomplishment—identity—and treat it as if it were the locus of truth and pure self-certainty; in effect, to treat it as if it could be withdrawn from the flux of being. Connolly locates the problem of evil and its origin at precisely this point, because as soon as the demand for truth and purity is installed in my identity, the world becomes populated by at least some differences that now constitute an incalculable threat to my security. This shift of perception and affect is identified by Connolly as a transforming of "difference into otherness." When such a transformation has occurred, then not merely some *particular actions* taken by another are a threat, but rather "the very visibility of its mode of *being* as other."[16]

Although this dynamic of identity and otherness might seem to play itself out essentially in the media of language and interaction, Connolly suggests that its intensity is inscribed upon the visceral register as well. Accordingly, he speaks of the "visceral register of subjectivity and intersubjectivity," by which he means that this dynamic produces a "corporealization of culture." As a result of this process, certain "others" can strike us as objects that just "naturally" evoke reactions of disgust, hostility, fear, and so on, because we immediately "recognize" them this way, rather than through some process of conscious reflection.[17]

I will have more to say later on the various ethical-political issues raised by this way of thinking about identity and otherness. For the moment, I want to return to what Connolly says starts the dynamics by which some differences are constituted as otherness. The culprit is the desire that my identity be stamped with a truth or self-certainty that somehow rises above or masters the flow of becoming. For Connolly, this desire is deeply rooted in Western civilization, at least since the rise of Christianity. But he thinks it is a desire that can be resisted and reworked if we can bring ourselves to unsettle the implicit or explicit, strong ontological foundations that continually feed that desire. A key mode by which we might initiate such change is to begin to knead experiences of the uncanny into something other than that which is shuffled aside or quickly defused by fixed moral categories, thereby fueling a resentment of those "others" who may seem to threaten us. We might let the anxiety evoked by the uncanny resonate more slowly and often, figuring this experience as testimony that the world may *not* be *for us,* may not answer—without violence—our desire for fixity in identity, morality, and masterful projects.

[16] *ID,* 66.

[17] *WNS,* 3; "Techniques of Thought," 6.

Its presencing is always excessive in relation to the various sorts of solidity and security we seek.[18]

But this figuring of the uncanny is not exhausted by its deflationary aspect. It is also affirmative in that the "nonteleological excess of being over identity" is experienced also *as* richness or abundance; in effect, as something given to us. It is that moment of experience that, for Connolly, fulfills the central role of ontological source. Here we feel and affirm an originary "beauty and energy" that can in turn evoke a "reverence" for, and "enchantment" with, the becoming of life. Moreover, it is important to cultivate such sentiments, because they alone are our resources for helping "us bear up under the pressures of contingency and bad luck"; bear up, that is, when the energy of becoming deals us terrible blows, and we are tempted to seek out "others" on whom to visit our resentment at what we take to be the unfairness of existence.[19]

Whether our cultivation of reverence and enchantment will have such an effect or not is something no one can guarantee. At bottom, there is nothing more than faith, both in this possible existential effect and in the fuller "ethical promise inside the experience of the uncanny." Connolly thus makes no effort to hide the contestability of the ethical implications of his ontology: "These are big articles of faith. About as big as the [theistic] ones they contest."[20]

5.1.B. Provisional or Weak?

Before turning directly to Connolly's efforts to flesh out the shape of the ethical promise of his ontology, I want to consider more carefully how he understands its status as ontology. In this regard, it is notable that he sometimes shies away from flatly describing his position as an ontology, preferring to say that it is an "ont*a*logy" or contains an "ontopolitical dimension." Although these locutions seem to indicate a basic skepticism about ontology, I would suggest that this skepticism is aimed only at strong ontologies. Connolly is here calling attention to his debt to Foucault. The latter affirms only an "anti-logical logos" or "a hypothetical, ont*a*logical universal, one designed to disturb the closure and narcissism of dogmatic identities, . . . and one treated as an alternative to ontologies of Law and Purpose."[21] Described in this fashion, an ont*a*logy looks rather like a strategic tool whose main purpose is to animate the con-

[18] *AI*, 136–38.
[19] *AI*, 14; *ID*, 81–82, 120–21; *WNS*, 16.
[20] *AI*, 126, 137; *ID*, 120.
[21] *EP*, 1; *AI*, 146.

struction of genealogies. It is hypothetical in the sense that *if* I want to critically unmask dogmatic identities, *then* I must employ some conceptual construct that provides guidance to the strategy of genealogy in a fashion analogous to the way strong ontology empowers certainty. This strategically deployed ont*a*logical frame is constituted when Foucault asserts that "Nothing is fundamental," and that "the intelligible appear[s] against a background of emptiness."[22]

Ont*a*logy thus appears to imply ontological affirmation in only a hypothetical, strategic sense. If this is the case, then Connolly's position is something less than a weak ontology. It would be somehow more "provisional," as one critic of poststructuralist efforts has put it.[23] But I think this actually misconstrues what Connolly is up to. His affirmation of a "protean vitality of being" does suggest the need for genealogical critiques of dogmatic identities and strong ontologies, but it is not itself "provisional" or simply strategic. Besides the Foucauldian debt, there is also a Nietzschean one that draws selectively upon the latter's appeal to a kind of vitalism.

Nietzsche, at least at one period of his life, affirmed the idea of either "an elemental energy directly accessible to experience by nonlinguistic means or . . . a vital purposive force that must be allowed expression regardless of the implications that it carries for anyone or anything else." Connolly's debt here is, importantly, a limited one; he specifically rejects any notions of a full and linguistically unmediated access to being and its purpose (and he thinks "the mature Nietzsche" did as well).[24] What remains is the idea of an ontological source that always exceeds any given interpretation, and this exceeding is itself interpreted as a giving of being, a generosity, to which we owe a peculiar kind of gratitude. To my mind, this source is affirmed by Connolly *wholeheartedly,* not strategically, provisionally, or at arm's length, for it is to the inspiriting force of such affirmation that we must look for motivational resources for our ethical-political life.[25] In sum, I think that when Connolly uses the term "ont*a*logy," it means roughly what weak ontology means, an interpretation of being that is not provisional or thin, but rather deeply affirmed and rich, yet ultimately contestable.

[22] Quoted in *AI,* 147, 150.

[23] Peter Digeser, *Our Politics, Our Selves: Liberalism, Identity, and Harm* (Princeton, N.J.: Princeton University Press, 1995), 134.

[24] *AI,* 146. Digeser sees Connolly as shifting uncertainly between two incompatible ideas of ontology: as something, provisional and as something prediscursive (*Our Politics, Our Selves,* 134–35). If I am right, Connolly embraces neither of these options.

[25] Connolly suggests that Foucault can also be interpreted as moving in this direction (*AI,* 147; *EP,* 32–40).

5.1.C. The Cultivation of Sensibility

When he turns to the interface of ethics and his ontology, Connolly stresses the centrality of cultivation and contestability. What he seeks is a way of envisioning cultivation that both pursues a "positive ethic," but continually manifests its own contingency in the pursuit itself; in short, an ethos that continually folds back upon the tendency of any perspective to gather a momentum toward certainty.

The notion of cultivation becomes central precisely because he is not articulating "a morality of contract or command." Rather the ethos he seeks to foster "exceed[s] any fixed codes of morality." Moreover, although it orients itself to the idea of cultivation, this activity is only partially related to traditional teleological conceptions of ethics, because the latter typically envision virtues as being cultivated against the background of some ontology of "intrinsic purpose." The sensibility Connolly seeks to cultivate will often "disturb traditional virtues" and the ontologies that anchor them. His ethic "does not present itself as the single universal to which other ethical traditions must bow." Instead "it provides a prod and counterpoint to them, pressing them to rethink" the way they should engage others who affirm different ethical sources.[26] Stated in this contestatory fashion, it begins to sound as though Connolly's ethos will pretty much cash itself out as a critical prod to its opponents, the upshot of which is that any positive component recedes into the ineffable realms of the "to come," as Derrida puts it.[27] But this familiar tack is not the one Connolly follows. His ethic never removes itself from the field of contestation, but it has a character that is not exhausted by its role as paladin of critique.

What then is the positive content of the sensibility he seeks to cultivate? It draws its shape from the figuration of unmanageable presencing as a richness or "fugitive abundance"; in short, a giving. To come to see-feel being in this way is to experience an awe or reverence that is alloyed with a sense of "*gratitude* for the rich abundance of life." This gratitude is " 'religious' " without being theistic, and it constitutes "a source of ethical inspiration." One expresses this gratitude by what one might call an *active* bearing-witness to being, which takes the form of a "protean care for the world" whose presencing always exceeds our efforts at framing, identifying, and grounding. Such care is manifested as an "ethos of generosity and forbearance."[28]

[26] *EP*, xxiv.

[27] Jacques Derrida, *Specters of Marx: The State of the Debt, the Work of Mourning, and the New International*, trans. P. Kamuf (New York: Routledge, 1994), 169.

[28] *EP*, xxiii, 28; *WNS*, 7, 54–55 (see also n. 12), 159.

I will consider how such an ethos informs political life in the following section; for the moment, I just want to give an initial sense of what it involves. First, one notices that Connolly uses the term *ethos* frequently in place of *ethics*. My sense is that he wants to emphasize continually that the orientation he seeks is vivified more by a spirit or sensibility than by any set rules of conduct. A generous sensibility in this sense is one receptive to the "possibilities of being imperfectly installed in established institutional practices." A key, underlying goal of ethical action is to enhance this receptivity in one's self and others. What this means for the self is a greater attentiveness to the visceral dimension of reflection and insight, as well as to one's tendency to transform difference into a hostile or threatening otherness. More broadly, it means that I engage the "play of identities, institutions, and principles," with the hope of "rendering them more responsive to that which exceeds them, more generous and refined in their engagement with difference."[29]

There is one other crucial initial component of the ethos Connolly admires, and that is the virtue of "forbearance."[30] Given his debt to Nietzsche and the lingering concerns about that philosopher's work in relation to the possible deleterious ethical-political implications of the idea of a "will to power," it is important to see that Connolly's ontology is not easily aligned with any pure assertion of will. At least in some places, Nietzsche would seem to endorse the image of an aristocratic warrior type, freed from the pettiness of resentment, and who proves himself in his free choice of opponents. This image can even accommodate the virtue of generosity, in the form of a kind of noble liberality. But forbearance would probably have to count for him at least partially as a "sick" virtue. Such is not the case with Connolly. Nietzsche's image of a self that attunes itself with the vitalistic thrusts of the *Weltwillen* (world will), would always be, within Connolly's ontology, a delusional projection.[31] A self centered on a pure will is as much of a delusion as the image of a fully detached self. Connolly's point about the multiple registers of cognition and viscerality is that any such image of purity is deceptive, a false promise of an immaculate self-control and disengagement. Similarly, the picture of a self cleansed of resentment who strolls disinterestedly into agonistic space to choose his opponents forgets that even the agent who succeeds in dampening his resentment has not thereby extricated his identity from the ontological dynamics of identity/difference. To do justice to this dynamic, one needs to exercise the virtue of forbearance in

[29] *AI*, 141.

[30] *WNS*, 7, 9.

[31] Friedrich Nietzsche, *The Birth of Tragedy*, trans. F. Golffing (New York: Doubleday, 1956), 103.

relations with others; in doing so, one affirms that "ambiguity of being" which always lodges traces of otherness within me.[32]

The forgoing points about cultivation and forbearance are also important to keep in mind when Connolly speaks sometimes of "self-artistry" rather than cultivation. Appeals to the self as a work of art sometimes seem to imply that one works with an infinite palate on a perfectly clean canvas. From what I have shown of Connolly's ontology, it should be clear that his use of the image of self-artistry does not carry such an implication. His self is a "modest artist" whose goal is "neither to *discover* a true self underneath . . . sedimented layers nor to *create* the self anew entirely by oneself." We are encouraged only to "work demurely on a relational self that has already been formed."[33]

5.2. The Ethos of "Agonistic Democracy"

A moment ago I touched on Connolly's affinity for the concept of ethos. This affinity is important to keep in mind when one assesses his efforts to rethink democratic theory. The heart of this rethinking is not adequately captured by any determinate principles of justice or institutional recommendations. His radicality does not lie in proposals for a wholesale transformation of the basic structures of liberal democracy, but rather for a "micropolitics" that might animate those structures differently.[34] Although Connolly's ethos intends to unsettle a good deal more than Taylor's, there is a certain parallel between them in the sense that the central issue for each is, as the latter puts it, exploring "different ways of living the political and economic structures that the contemporary age makes mandatory."[35]

In this section, I want to consider first the issue of ontological prefiguration; that is, how and what Connolly's "post-Nietzschean sensibility" prefigures ethically and politically. This prefiguration is guided partially by the specific ontological figures I have elucidated and partially by the exigencies that are foregrounded by Connolly's "grand narrative" of late modernity (section 5.2.A). Connolly would claim that the most distinctive ethical-political bearing that is prefigured is a generosity toward emergent political identities and movements that he calls "critical responsiveness" (section 5.2.B). After sketching this idea, I develop a critique of it that takes issue less with this bearing itself than with the way

[32] *WNS,* 160–61; cf. *EP,* 188. Connolly speaks of "the constitutive experience of uncertainty and instability in the will" (*WNS,* 12). See also his thoughts on Nietzsche in this regard (*WNS,* 52ff).

[33] *WNS,* 145–46, 150.

[34] *WNS,* 148.

[35] Taylor, *PA,* xii.

Connolly would have us understand its relation to his ontology. I also take up here the challenge that Taylor offers to any ethical-political perspective that draws its sustenance from an "external, amoral" source (section 5.2.C). Next I turn to how critical responsiveness fits into a broader "ethos of engagement" with already established contestants on the political landscape. The force of this ethos is intended to unsettle the secular modus vivendi of the liberal democratic state, as well as its subtle attachment to the value of nationhood (section 5.2.D). I consider finally how all this challenges some core ideas of political liberalism (section 5.2.E).

5.2.A. Gratitude for Fugitive Abundance

The foregoing, initial sketch of a "protean care for the world" already brings with it the issue of prefiguration. How exactly are we to be moved from the brute idea of unmanageable presencing to the richness or abundant "giving" of being; and, further, to a diffuse care for life; and then, finally, to a specific ethos of democracy? Connolly's sense of this movement fits, I would suggest, within the terms of my notion of the way a weak ontology should prefigure an ethics and politics. He emphasizes repeatedly that the steps from ontology to a democratic ethos are "neither certain nor necessary."[36] Moreover, the movement from any one step to another has both cognitive and affective dimensions. Connolly's language for describing this movement is particularly helpful. To speak more cognitively, one step "enables [another] as a possibility and disarms certain kinds of objections and resistances to that possibility." To speak more affectively, one step provides "intimations" and "inspiration" for moving to another.[37]

The initial figuration of unmanageable presencing can be solicited, as I showed earlier, from the fleeting experience of the uncanny. As I also indicated, the succeeding step to being as fugitive abundance implies that one has somehow come to take being as a kind of giving that has no giver behind it. But exactly what considerations animate this further figuring of being? At this point one can see that Connolly's ontology is itself partially prefigured by a grand historical narrative. Recall that when he speaks of our experience of the "rich *an-arche* of being," he calls it a "*late modern* experience" (my emphasis). Now what is there about late

[36] *ID*, 167; cf. "Rethinking *The Ethos of Pluralization*," *Philosophy and Social Criticism* 24, no. 1 (1998): 99 (This essay is part of a symposium on *EP*); *EP*, 1, 16.

[37] "Rethinking *The Ethos of Pluralization*," 98; *ID*, 81, 167. In an exchange with me (part of the symposium cited in n. 36), Connolly indicates that he is not certain that my sense of "prefigure" coincides with his understanding of the relation of ontology to the ethical-political. But, given my understanding of his further elucidation of his own sense of the relation, I do not see any significant divergence of views; see "Rethinking," 98.

modernity that might motivate a reading of unmanageable presencing *as* a rich giving, toward which one in turn responds with a kind of gratitude?

For Connolly, a central characteristic of Western modernity has been the presence of a "compensatory code of secular reassurance" that has helped us to domesticate somewhat the prospect of death with no immortality. This code has taken shape as the persistent, underlying presumption of, "first, a close alignment between the identity the self seeks to realize and socially available possibilities of formation and, second, a shared sense of confidence in the world we are building." If Western modernity is the time in which these expectations, despite periodic deflations, have remained robust, then late modernity might be defined as the time in which they have become permanently unsettled. Connolly names three accelerating uncertainties as the culprits. First, there is today "an intensification of the experience of owing one's life and destiny to world-historical, national, and local-bureaucratic forces." Second, there is "a decline in the confidence many constituencies have in the probable future to which they find themselves contributing in daily life." Third, there is the growth of problems at a global level which increasingly seem beyond the capacity of even the most powerful of nation states to solve. Flows of capital and populations, the availability of natural resources, environmental degradation, the threat of nuclear terrorism, the upsurge of ethnic and national identifications, to name a few, all increasingly produce heightened anxiety for our modern imaginary within which nation states are the presumed "site of collective freedom and mastery."

The combined impact of these three phenomena evokes a new set of insights and affective propensities.

> In late modernity, the contingency of life and the fragility of things become more vivid and compelling, while reflection on the issues posed by this condition is shuffled to the margins of state-centered discourse. Established disciplines and rules become experienced more often as arbitrary restraints insecurely linked to the future that justifies them. Resentment becomes more generalized and acute, and more actively seeks available targets of vilification. Politics becomes less attuned to the future and more locked into claims of the present, less attentive to claims of the suffering and more willing to discipline those whose suffering cannot be ignored. The late-modern condition compromises the individual's bond of affection to the common life, disciplines individuality, disconnects present decisions from care about the future they engender, and disrupts stable contexts in which the ambiguous exercise of freedom occurs.[38]

[38] *ID*, 25–26.

These effects crystallize in the intensification of an underlying tension that has always been part of the character of modern pluralist democracies. Such polities by their very nature experience friction between the imperative of protecting the economic and cultural conditions of the distribution of identities existing at any given time, on the one hand, and the imperative of openness to the emergence of new identities, on the other. But the conditions of late modernity bring with them an intensification of this tension, out of which emerge, in turn, two persistent, contending responses. First, there is an accelerated drive for further "cultural *pluralization*"; and second, there is a more "aggressive *fundamentalization* of existing identities."[39] It is this heightened tension that provides the most basic terms today for ontological, ethical and political reflection.

On the ontological level, the drive toward fundamentalization reinvigorates the appeal of strong ontologies, with their promise of a secure home and higher purpose, to which one can attach unquestioned loyalty, as projects of mastery are thrown into question. Strains of such fundamentalization are found in the resurgence of religious fundamentalism, and in some variants of nationalism, communitarianism, and deep ecology. For Connolly, all of these responses are inadequate to the current challenge. They are too steeped in a nostalgia for what has been lost to be able either to confront imaginatively the growing sense of contingency in late modern life, or to contest effectively the tendency to reinflate continually the modern confidence in mastery.

Now Connolly is aware that such arguments on his part have no knock-down power, especially against a sophisticated "attunement" perspective, such as Taylor's. He hopes merely to sow enough doubt to create some space for the "introduction of a perspective that disturbs both the mastery project and the attunement dissent."[40] It is within this historically situated space of reflection that Connolly detects a widespread sense of cognitive and aesthetic-affective dissatisfaction that can find some reorientation through a distinctive sort of ontological figuration. When unmanageable presencing is figured as fugitive abundance or richness, it constitutes an ontological source that may, Connolly hopes, provide some spiritual sustenance, as do ontologies of attunement, without, however, projecting an intrinsic purpose into being.

But the attractiveness of such a figuration of an ontological source would have to imply something like a need for sustenance of this sort. This particular need cannot itself have the status of an existential universal, because its emergence in this form is made a possibility only within

[39] *EP,* 97, 100; "Rethinking *The Ethos of Pluralization,*" 94.
[40] *EP,* 24.

a specific historical context, in which neither mastery nor theistic attunement encounters a deep resonance in substantial numbers of people. But one's specific susceptibility to the appeal of being as fugitive abundance is rooted finally in what does seem to function as an existential universal for Connolly: "the attachment to existence . . . installed in life," a fervent cathexis that "flows deeper" than the imperatives of "will, consciousness, and identity." As an existential universal, this stubborn "drive to life" is essentially underdetermined; that is, it can find articulation in a variety of onto-political directions.[41] Connolly's overall point then would be to urge that in the circumstances of late modernity this fervent attachment can find edifying articulation in the figuration of being as fugitive abundance. The cultivation of a sense of the world's rich giving might, in turn, make for a life today that would seem less besieged and resentment-prone than one attuned to either a transcendent purpose or the hopes of eventual mastery.

The cultivation of such an ontological bent also prepares the way for an articulation of that "ethos of generosity" that I spoke of earlier. Just as with all the other stages of prefiguration, the way toward the latter is no philosophically royal road, but rather one that has "irreducible gaps and openings." Thus, a generous "care for the protean diversity of life," although it certainly resonates with the figure of richness, cannot fail to acknowledge its status as, at least partially, a free "gift."[42] When I introduced the idea of this ethos in section 5.1, I referred to it as an *active* bearing-witness to being. Perhaps I can specify this more precisely now. The actions that are engendered by such an ethos of generosity are a form of participating in being in a way that is distinctive to humans. The sense of participation I have in mind here is roughly analogous to Heidegger's *Gelassenheit,* although that notion seems to imply the affirmation of only the most "delicate" of actions. Heidegger speaks of the poet's exquisitely light bringing of things to presence in poetic speech. In that activity one mimes or participates in being by calling something into the world in speech, and yet this thing is not grasped and put into a frame of systematic use.[43] Connolly also wants to animate action that is a kind of miming of being. But given his ontology's thematization of the visceral dimension and the constitutive dynamic of human identity/difference, the sort of participation he affirms will be less exquisitely beautiful and unsullied, as well as more socially engaged, assertive, and risky.

[41] *AI,* 81–82, 168–70; *WNS,* 160; "Rethinking *The Ethos of Pluralization,*" 98.

[42] *EP,* 40, 93; "Rethinking *The Ethos of Pluralization,*" 99.

[43] See my discussion of this theme in Heidegger in *Political Theory and Postmodernism,* 67 ff.

Connolly's figuration of being as fugitive abundance suggests to him the need to cultivate a wide repertoire of ways to work on oneself. These arts aim to aid us in thinking and feeling life in accord with that ontological source. But he picks out one effect of this cultivation that has a distinctive significance; this he calls "critical responsiveness to the politics of becoming."[44] One of the strongest and most intriguing aspects of Connolly's work is the way in which it carefully teases out the character of such an ethos of responsiveness to the natality of human being. Gestures in this general direction are quite familiar among contemporary thinkers who have been influenced by postmodern or poststructuralist insights. Butler, as I have shown, does something of this sort in her appeal to a stance of generosity toward becoming (see section 4.3.B). Connolly, however, takes us beyond general appeals and gestures to extended sketches of both the shape of "critical responsiveness" and how it is to be located in relation to a variety of specific, traditional concerns of political theory.

5.2.B. Critical Responsiveness to the Politics of Becoming

> The most admirable arts of the self cultivate the capacity for critical responsiveness in a world in which the politics of becoming periodically poses surprises to the self-interpretations of established constituencies.[45]

The "politics of becoming" is Connolly's term for the process of disturbance and enactment by which new identities and movements emerge into public life. This process is never frictionless in the sense that it always challenges the identities and place of those groups and sectors of the population that already have "standing" in the public sphere. And such friction is a traditional part of a pluralist democracy's official self-understanding of the character of political life. But this formal awareness that one must learn to live with the disturbance implied by pluralization is countered by a less conscious "inertia of presumption" that constantly reconstrues established identities and social norms as essentially affiliated with "Nature, God, Law, or Purpose." This kind of inertia is what gives rise to the tendency to celebrate a society's openness, as expressed in recognition of the last constituency that has struggled into the circle of establishment, but to oppose a similar status for a currently emerging movement because "*they* are different." Connolly has in mind here, for example, the way some conservative, white, Christian groups in the United States in the 1990s, began to trumpet their newfound love for

[44] "Rethinking *The Ethos of Pluralization*," 98.
[45] *WNS*, 146; *EP*, 180.

African-Americans, but took a determinately hostile stance toward gays and lesbians.[46]

To a degree, this underlying desire for a "politics of forgetfulness" has always haunted pluralism; but, under the conditions of late modernity, Connolly suggests that it has become more pervasive and insistent. It is here that he warns about the growing force of fundamentalization today, and urges us to explore ways of slackening it. "Critical responsiveness" is the name he gives to the mode of sensibility we need to cultivate in order to begin to address this problem.

The sense of critical responsiveness emerges from asking the question: what sensibility toward the phenomena of politics will best express or "flow from" the diffuse ethos of generous care for a world of fugitive abundance?[47] If the drive to fundamentalize expresses a desire to freeze the irruptive contingency of political life, critical responsiveness would express a desire both to reimagine this specific mode of unruliness as richness and to participate with generosity in the process of political natality. This responsiveness constitutes a participation in being in a way that continually commemorates the ontological figuration of presencing and abundance. Such participation is an active giving-way-to the natality of political identity. It shares with Heidegger's *Gelassenheit* a forbearance that lets things come into being, but this giving-way-to also requires a more activist turn to political life, because it must intervene in the dynamic play of identities and practices in order to resist tendencies to fundamentalize or freeze this play in accordance with the self-interpretation of established constituencies. The giving-way-to of critical responsiveness is thus also always to some degree a making-way-for emergent movements in political space.

Once critical responsiveness has been shown to be at the core of a more generous pluralism, Connolly possesses a distinctive perspective from which to construe the value of a variety of strategies typically associated with Nietzsche and Foucault. Thus, genealogical analysis becomes useful in thawing the hard surfaces of the politics of forgetfulness, thereby making possible cognitive and affective space for greater openness to the politics of enactment. By itself, however, genealogy does not directly elicit the sensibility of critical responsiveness. That role is filled by a variety of "techniques" or "arts of the self," the effect of which is to "install" this distinctive generosity "in the feelings." The general notion of the self as a work of art, as it has been employed by followers of Nietzsche and Foucault, has sometimes seemed to be at the heart of what critics of postmodernism find to be a philosophy of pure, boundless self-

[46] *AI,* 148–50.
[47] *EP,* 187.

creation. Even if this charge is valid in some cases, it does not hit the mark in the case of Connolly. His self is viscerally dense and culturally entangled. Thus, as I noted earlier, its work is always modest and incremental. It experiments with a variety of techniques and tactics: one "shuffle[s] back and forth between intensities, feelings, images, smells and concepts, modifying some of them and the relays between them," opening up thereby "the possibility of new thinking and modified sensibilities," without ever being in complete control of these effects. And, of course, in applying such techniques and tactics, one is also articulating—in Taylor's sense—an ontological source that continually reanimates these specific efforts by expanding "little spaces of joy and generosity already there so as to cultivate the spirit necessary to respond creatively and generously to political movements that cast universal pretensions of this or that aspect of your identity into doubt." One is thus continually drawn to desanctify elements in one's identity, so they do not succumb to the pull of fundamentalization.[48]

On the basis of what has been said, it should be obvious that Connolly's self-artistry is not a solitary aesthetics, but rather always already a "micropolitics" in the sense of cultivating a sensibility that is continually informing, and informed by, your ethical-political interactions. And it is the practice of such a micropolitics of critical responsiveness that is necessary to engender a pluralism more generous than one operating only with more traditional liberal understandings of tolerance and justice.[49]

In order to develop this claim, Connolly makes use of the metaphor of a threshold that emerging political movements have to pass before they become full candidates for public life, to which one owes tolerance and justice. In this regard, critical responsiveness does bear a certain "family resemblance to liberal tolerance," but the latter promotes "forbearance to established constituencies diverging from your faith and identity," whereas the former involves a greater attentiveness to the difficulties and suffering that occur as a relatively inchoate force of becoming struggles toward the threshold of establishment as a movement.[50]

For Connolly, liberal conceptions of justice, such as Rawls's, which forgo any thematization of sensibility and self-artistry, fail to see that "a whole lot of micropolitical preparation" has to occur before suffering below the threshold of recognition is interpreted as having crossed over it. It is a question here of "modes of being consciously or unconsciously shuffled below normal personhood" and thus below the level of a full bearer of rights. Liberal justice tends to underestimate the momentum

[48] *AI,* 144–45; *WNS,* 145–46, 150–51, 176.

[49] *WNS,* 148.

[50] *WNS,* 62; "Rethinking *The Ethos of Pluralization,*" 95.

of inattentiveness, resistance, and resentment exhibited by established constituencies to the stirrings of new political identity from within the depths of what appear to be only "obscure pains, objective disorders, low levels of energy, perverse sexualities, basic inferiorities, uncivilized habits, hysterical symptoms, inherent abnormalities, and unreliable work dispositions."[51]

When one thinks from within the perspective of the politics of becoming and critical responsiveness, the process of progressively expanding the scope of rights over the last two centuries in the United States is given new cast.

> [S]laves were said to be inhabited by natural incapacities that pushed them below the threshold of full persons; John Brown, the abolitionist, was widely declared to be a monomaniac, a type, I believe, no longer recognized in the official nosology of psychiatry; women were said to be equipped for the immediate ethics of family life but not for the abstract deliberation essential to public life; atheists were (and still often are) said (e.g. by Tocqueville and the America he registered) to be too materialistic, narcissistic and selfish to hold public office, though each was person enough to participate in employment, commerce and military liability; "homosexuals" were (and often are) said to deserve justice as persons *and* to be marked by an objective disorder and/or sin shuffling their sensualities below the reach of justice; "post-modernists"—occupying today the subject position previously reserved for atheists—are said to be cool, amoral, and nihilistic, lacking the pre-requisites to be taken seriously as moral agents; doctors who assist terminally ill patients die were (and often are) defined as murderers because of the generic Christian injunction against taking one's own life; and Rawls himself now treats the mentally retarded as something less than full persons because they cannot participate fully in the practice of "fair cooperation" upon which his scheme of justice rests. In these cases either significant changes in interpretation of the extent to which the parties measure up to the existing code of personhood or changes in the implicit composition of personhood itself were needed. In most cases both were required. And in no case is either argument or the establishment of simple facts, previously overlooked, sufficient to the change. In each case a shift in sensibility informs the changes in interpretation and composition.[52]

Such shifts in sensibility can be engendered by consciously applied tactics of the self. Consider, for example, the issue of doctor-assisted suicide, as it is being thrashed out in contemporary American politics. At issue is the claim to a new right that is not recognized generally in Ameri-

[51] *WNS,* 69, 140.
[52] *WNS,* 67.

can law. Proponents of such a right argue that we are failing to acknowledge adequately an extreme form of suffering, and we are denying those who are suffering a right to choose to end it. From those who find such claims offensive or simply not compelling, critical responsiveness requires some work on the self. Connolly imagines a possible scenario of self-artistry for engaging this whole issue:

> Suppose you habitually assume that death must come when God or nature brings it. A new political movement by those who claim the right to doctor assisted death when people are in severe pain or terminally ill shocks you to the core. You concur with those critics who accuse the doctors of death of cruelty to the dying, of self indulgence, and of a lack of respect for the fundamental design of being. But, later, when the shock of the new demand wears away a little, your concern for the suffering of the dying in a world of high-tech medical care opens a window to exploration of other possibilities. *One part of your subjectivity now begins to work on other parts.* In this case your concern for those who writhe in agony as they approach death may work on assumptions of divinity or nature already burned into your being. But how to proceed? Cautiously. Perhaps you attend a film in which the prolonged suffering of a dying person becomes palpable. Or you talk with friends who have gone through this arduous experience with parents who pleaded for help to end their suffering. Next you expose yourself to a larger variety of understandings of divinity and nature than you had previously entertained. These two activities in tandem may enable you to appreciate more vividly the significant shifts in such conceptions that have already swept across western history. So perhaps the current organization of your instincts in this domain is not the last word after all. Then you re-encounter the high-tech world of medical care, reliving as you do distressing images of your father struggling with pain when he died of pancreatic cancer. You now visualize more starkly how contemporary medical practice often splits into distinct parts elements heretofore taken to constitute the unity of death itself. The brain may die while the heart still beats. Or the possibility of participating in cultural life may disappear while other signs of life persist. Or intense pain may make the end of life intolerable to bear. Through the conjunction of these diverse modalities of intervention changes in the thinking behind your thoughts may now begin to form. Some elements in your experience of nature and morality may now clash more actively with others. Or perhaps you still find your previous conception of nature to be persuasive. But uncertainties and paradoxes attached to it combine with a more intensive appreciation of contemporary dilemmas of medical care to encourage you to try to desanctify that interpretation to a greater degree. You continue to affirm, say, a teleological conception of nature in which the purposiveness of death is set, but now you acknowledge how this judgment may be more contestable than you

> had previously appreciated. And you begin to feel this uncertainty more intensely as a conflict within yourself. You even begin to wonder whether your previous refusal to allow others to die as they determine (when such determinations are possible) might have contained a desire to preserve a reassuring interpretation of the wholeness of nature even more than a concern for their dignity or well-being. What was heretofore nonnegotiable gradually becomes rethinkable. You now register more actively the importance of giving presumptive respect to the judgment of the sufferer in this domain, even when that judgment calls into question in a disturbing way your own conception of nature, death or divinity. Eventually, through personal communications and public engagements, you bring some of these considerations to others with whom you are associated, seeking to spur them to similar bouts of reappraisal.[53]

Connolly would certainly not claim that there is any necessity in this scenario, either as to specific tactics or end point. He would claim, however, that we are obliged to undertake such work on the self, and that the character of this work is not simply a matter of cognitively sorting through a stack of arguments pro and con. The artistry involves rather a moving back and forth from the cognitive to the aesthetic-affective in several registers: "working now on thought-imbued feelings, then on thought-imbued intensities below the reach of feeling, now on received images of death and suffering, again on intensive memories of suffering, and then on entrenched concepts of divinity, identity, ethics and nature."[54] One nudges this process forward carefully and experimentally, never quite knowing in advance where it will lead.

5.2.C. Some Criticisms

With the foregoing characterization of critical responsiveness in place, I want to now raise some questions about that ethos and the ontology to which it is linked. First, I will suggest that there are some significant problems with the prefigurative links that Connolly constructs. Second, since Connolly's project affirms what Taylor calls an external, amoral source, I will take up the latter's assertion that any such project inevitably entangles itself with violence.

With regard to the prefiguration problem, what I want to suggest is that the central ontological figure of abundance, by itself, inadequately prefigures the ethical qualities Connolly assigns to critical responsiveness. The difficulty emerges at the point where Connolly wishes to

[53] *WNS*, 146–47.
[54] *WNS*, 147–48.

draw us from the "protean care" for the sheer presencing or becoming of *being as such* to a more focused, obligating care for *human* being. This is the crucial step toward critical responsiveness. Now neither Connolly nor I would want to contend that any rational necessity is involved in such a step. Nevertheless, a felicitous ontological figuration should, I think, provide more persuasive pointers at this critical moment of entanglement of the ontological and ethical-political. In short, Connolly is taking us in a normative direction toward which his ontology has not given enough orientation. This deficit shows up in two places.

First, how does Connolly draw us to a special preference for, and attention to, *human* presencing over any other dimensions of the presencing of being? In short, why support the occurrence of, say, a gay and lesbian rally in a local park, rather than its suppression, something one might prefer on the basis of enjoying the unobstructed greening of the vegetation in the park. This example might strike one as far-fetched. But I think ultimately Heidegger's *later* ethical-political reflections had difficulties rooted in this issue.[55] My point here is not to tar Connolly with the brush of Heideggerian politics, but to call attention to a place in his argument from which others could plausibly proceed from similar ontological figures in directions he would deeply oppose. Without asking for an ironclad, rational warranty for the avoidance of a Heideggerian path, one can still press the question: Can't Connolly provide us with a more careful prefiguration here?

The second issue concerns not just distinguishing between presencing per se and human presencing, but rather the problem of drawing distinctions between different modes of human presencing; more particularly between those that injure human equality and dignity, and those that affirm or embody them. An ontology the heart of which resides in the sense of an inexhaustible abundance of being does not by itself offer an adequate prefiguration of this crucial ethical distinction. The unwarranted link in Connolly's ontopolitical configuration occurs when the simple idea of abundance or diversity is taken as an adequate ontological prefiguration of the idea of a political world open to a politics of becoming. The problem here is that the sheer richness of human being

[55] I am thinking here, for example, of Heidegger's presentation of his essay "Building, Dwelling, Thinking" in the bomb-ravaged city of Darmstadt in 1946. What this paper implied was that the audience in this devastated city was being superficial if its members worried too much about the mere everyday sense of dwelling—having a roof over one's head—rather than about the more admirable sense of dwelling he had in mind: a proper openness to the presencing or event of being. Cf. Richard Bernstein, "Heidegger's Silence? Ethos and Technology," in *The New Constellation: The Ethical-Political Horizons of Modernity/Postmodernity* (Cambridge: MIT Press, 1992), 132.

could perhaps be as well realized in phenomena of repression and suppression as it would be in pluralization. We clearly recognize this in the psychological life of individuals. If experiential richness is all we are concerned with, then perhaps severe neurosis has much to offer. A parallel argument on the collective level has been made by Polish writer and poet Czeslaw Milosz, who asserted in the 1950s that authoritarian political rule can actually engender a certain sort of rich and resourceful consciousness.[56]

My point then is that the ontological figuration of abundance is too radically underdetermined to prefigure *by itself* all the qualities Connolly wants to include in the ethical attitude of critical responsiveness. That attitude, which would have us be attentive to that which is abject, marginalized, denigrated, in need, and so on, is intended to carry with it a clear sensitivity to the distinction between the abundance of human presencing per se and presencing that calls us to respect equal dignity. In effect, one could say that critical responsiveness can take the form it does for Connolly only if some ontological work is assumed within this configuration as a whole for which he has not given us an accounting.

One way to bring what is missing here into greater relief is to reconsider the way Connolly conceptualizes justice. Justice for him, as for Foucault, is narrowly construed as a "code" that resonates with the values of command and discipline. Within this genealogized understanding, justice remains a crucial value in Connolly's project, but one that is clearly subordinate to the ethos of critical responsiveness. The latter is what engenders a receptiveness to new political initiatives that Connolly sees as necessary for opening up orthodox pluralism, which, as presently constituted, is overly fixated on accommodating already established political movements within codes of justice. Critical responsiveness, then, must be understood to be "more fundamental than justice."[57]

Now this does not mean that Connolly in any sense denigrates the value of justice. In fact, he recognizes that "Justice and critical responsiveness are . . . bound together in a relation of dissonant interdependence." This relation, however, is one between a more fundamental and a less fundamental value. This sense is expressed by the threshold metaphor. Referring to the coming to presence of a new political constituency, Connolly speaks of "a place under-justice" where an ethics of critical responsiveness operates alone to facilitate the emergence of a social movement upward onto the "register of justice/injustice."[58]

[56] Czeslaw Milosz, *The Captive Mind,* trans. J. Zielonko (New York: Vintage, 1953), chap. 3.

[57] *EP,* 187.

[58] *EP,* 186–87.

> Each pluralizing movement, if and as it succeeds, migrates from an abject, abnormal, subordinate, or obscure Other *subsisting* in a nether world *under* the register of justice to a positive identity now *existing* on the register of justice/injustice. It is only after a movement crosses this critical threshold of identification that its injuries can acquire the standing of injustice or illegitimacy. This reveals the essential ambiguity of justice: the practice of justice is both indispensable after the crossing and a barrier to enactment before it. Critical responsiveness midwifes pluralizing movements across this critical threshold.[59]

This asymmetrical interdependence Connolly envisions is necessary because justice-as-code is not only blind, but also in a sense deaf and dumb. Modern conceptions of justice emerged in conjunction with the idea of a social contract. Justice is applicable to and binding upon rational, responsible parties. Connolly's point is that justice is *responsive* only *after* the status question is answered as to who is a recognizable participant. Thus, the sensitivities carried by the value of justice "miss the most critical and precarious moment in the *politics* of enactment."[60]

Connolly, to my mind, is onto something of real significance with this concern. He is correct to emphasize that a commitment to the value of justice does not engender the full ethical sensibility necessary for a radicalized pluralism. One needs "a bi-valent ethical sensibility" here: justice *and* something like critical responsiveness.[61]

Although I thus agree a good bit with Connolly on this issue, he nevertheless buries a significant problem for himself when he construes justice so narrowly, as "code." Such a conceptualization occludes another one that is perfectly familiar in ordinary language use: my doing justice to others. This diffuse and uncertain sense of obligation is not adequately captured by adherence to any political code. It does, however, seem to be roughly related to our distinctive character as *language* animals. One does not normally think of doing justice to plants or nonhuman animals, but rather to humans and their texts, taken in the broadest sense. Perhaps one can give a weak ontological interpretation of this contour of our moral language use by saying that it is prefigured in the distinctive way human being participates in the presencing of being.

Once again, a glance toward Heidegger may be useful. One thing that always fascinated him was the question of the distinctive human role in the presencing of being. Humans, of course, are conscious and can come to understand being in terms of presencing and adopt a reverential attitude based on that understanding of their *Dasein.* But there is a more

[59] *EP,* 184.
[60] *EP,* 184.
[61] *WNS,* 68.

active role that adheres to our capacity for language; we can not only witness presencing but also in some sense enact it, by bringing new complexes of meaning to life. As is well known, when it came to giving this ontological distinctiveness an ethical-political sense, Heidegger initially could do no better than dream of great *Staatsmänner* (statesmen) who could enact grand projects in ways unsullied by everyday human concerns. That dream went sour, of course, in the 1930s, leaving as satisfactory models of enactment only "poets" and "thinkers"—elevated characters who were also, in Heidegger's mind, above the noise, emotions, and "chatter" of everyday life.[62]

It seems to me that one can appropriate this ontological figuration of enactment without, at the same time, buying into Heidegger's peculiar longing for what is rare and elevated above ordinary life. Enactment becomes, accordingly, an everyday matter inextricably enmeshed with the symbolic expression of needs, suffering, identity, hopes, and so on. With enactment figured in this fashion, one has also prefigured the sense of doing justice to human beings in a particular fashion. One does justice, first, by recognizing the capacity of the other to participate distinctively in being through the disclosure of meaning; and, second, by appreciating the necessity of giving space to this disclosure of meaning, in the sense of allowing the possible novelty in the emergent symbolic complex to take shape. Finally, the peculiar natality of language that one should bear witness to here is not simply the production of meaning in an isolated utterance or other symbolic complex; rather it is this disclosure *as* the articulation of an ontological source. It is such a capacity for disclosure and articulation that best construes what human dignity amounts to, and thus that to which we owe justice.

We have now an ontological figuration of that peculiar quality of human being toward which our intuitions about "doing justice to" might reasonably be seen as directed. The addition of this dimension to Connolly's perspective would relieve it of the deficits in prefiguration which I have identified. (The deficit problem will emerge again later, though, in section 5.2.E.) And, to my mind, this modification could be accepted by him as a friendly amendment. Connolly, however, has responded skeptically to this suggestion that he rethink the prefigurative path to critical responsiveness. He contends rather that all one needs is a strong sense of generosity or "gift-giving" in order to be drawn over the gap between his ontology and his ethos of critical responsiveness.[63] But I am not con-

[62] Cf. the discussion of this issue in my *Political Theory and Postmodernism*, chaps. 3–4.

[63] "Rethinking *The Ethos of Pluralization*," 99. Connolly is drawing here on Romand Coles's *Rethinking Generosity: Critical Theory and the Politics of Caritas* (Ithaca, N.Y.: Cornell University Press, 1997).

vinced that it makes good sense to try to squeeze so much out of generosity alone. One's generosity always needs to be oriented in terms of when and toward what it is to be exercised. The formulation I just offered of "doing justice to" is not one that allows you to derive any specific obligations, and thereby bypass the need for generosity. This virtue remains crucial, just as it must be in any weak ontology.

I want to turn now to what is potentially a far more damaging criticism of Connolly. His perspective draws its sustenance from what Taylor calls an external, amoral source. And if this is so, then, according to Taylor, that perspective cannot resist a certain pull toward violence. This tendency is rooted in the peculiar combination of an urge to respond to something beyond life and a disavowal of any purpose to being. The rejection of any transcendent purpose transforms the urge toward the beyond human into a fascination "with the negation of life, with death and suffering."[64]

Connolly's views do indeed seem to appeal to an external, amoral source. First of all, he understands his source as something external, something beyond human life in the sense of its not being a pure artifact of human choice.[65] Our experience of that source may be historically conditioned, but it is not something we simply decide, at arm's length, to turn on or off. Connolly would, I think, agree with Taylor here that we always already have been "had" by some figuration of an ontological source. We may work ourselves into eventual disenchantment with any given figuration, but such work, conscious and unconscious, is poorly described as pure choice.

Connolly's ontological source is, moreover, amoral in Taylor's sense. His "late modern experience of the rich *an-archy* of being" portrays being as without transcendent moral purpose. Connolly's ontological source is that mobile, elusive, unmanageable presencing of things in the world that is "beyond good and evil." Life has no intrinsic moral vindication; it is simply "the fugitive experience standing at the end of the vindication line."[66]

If Connolly is thus an appropriate target for Taylor's critique, it remains now to ask whether the critique does in fact strike this particular target successfully. Recall that Taylor's concern is, broadly, to locate the danger that emerges with Nietzsche and continues to adhere to the projects of his successors down through Foucault. Recall also that Taylor dubs

[64] Taylor, "The Immanent Counter-Enlightenment," paper presented to Castelgandolfo Colloquium VII, August 1996, 9; and "Spirituality of Life and Its Shadow," *Compass* 14 no. 2 (1996): 4.

[65] Connolly specifically adopts Taylor's usage of the concept of sources, (*AI,* 141–43).

[66] *ID,* 170.

this tradition the "immanent counter-Enlightenment." The specific character of its discontent manifests itself in a revolt against the Enlightenment's according too much primacy to ordinary, mundane life. This revolt heaps scorn upon what it sees as the flattened, deadened world of the "herd" or bourgeois society, or the normalized individual. The rebels look to the redemptive power of an external source, whose influence upon us is to be felt aesthetically rather than morally. We are called to an aesthetic affirmation of an amoral vibrancy of being, a vibrancy that includes death and destruction. And here we engender as well, according to Taylor, a potential "fascination" with violence.[67]

Some would no doubt argue that Taylor is simply wrong in his attribution of this characteristic to the Nietzschean tradition. But I want to proceed as if there is some truth to the charge; and then consider whether Connolly shares as well in the guilt.

Perhaps the most plausible way to pursue the claim of co-conspiracy is to attend to the common theme of existential resentment. For Nietzsche, the overcoming of *ressentiment* requires a flight from the ordinary, from the herd and its moral rigorism, toward the ideal of the pure self-fashioning of the "overman" *(Ubermensch).* My suspicion is that if Taylor's claim about Nietzsche is right, the key to the problem lies in the peculiar combination of this distancing gesture with the vocation of self-artistry. From such a distance, violence and death might appear as intense but strangely unaffecting phenomena; in short, as objects that may fascinate but that remain detached from me.

On this reading of Taylor's charge, it is difficult to see how it could apply to Connolly. Although the latter is engaged with existential resentment, his resistance to it involves no radical distancing from ordinary life. One is urged to work on the self in order to dampen tendencies expressed in ordinary life, such as the marginalization of the uncanny and the propensity to transform difference into otherness; but this cultivation and its effects transpire in the realm of the everyday. Connolly describes his strategy as one of trying "to fold Nietzschean agonism into the fabric of ordinary life by attending to the extraordinary character of the latter."[68]

If fascination with violence and indifference to suffering do not arise from some sort of distancing from the ordinary, then perhaps it can be traced to the way in which Connolly handles finitude. As Taylor contends, a perspective such as Connolly's manifests "a bent to respond to something beyond" mere life, but since it possesses no concept of transcendence, it has a tendency to be drawn toward death as a "privileged per-

[67] "The Immanent Counter-Enlightenment," 10–12.

[68] *ID,* 187. Connolly sees himself as following Foucault in this regard.

spective."[69] Taylor is, I think, correct that one's mortality or finitude will be of central significance in a view such as Connolly's. But to admit that the cultivation of finitude without theism is crucial is not yet to admit that one thereby necessarily also toys with violence and ignores suffering.

A persistent engagement with one's finitude is paramount for Connolly, because one cannot otherwise affirm being as fugitive abundance. The task is to cultivate a fervent attachment to life without letting that fervency deceive itself into thinking it can finally apprehend the fugitive by gestures either of mastery or attunement with a transcendental source. But to do that, one must continually weave an acceptance of finitude into one's life. Taken in this light, the ethos of critical responsiveness constitutes a resource for the recollection of finitude. One simultaneously dampens the urge to purity, mastery, and self-certainty and enlivens a sensitivity to, and participation in, a process of natality whose character always remains beyond one's existing frames of interpretation.

Critical responsiveness is thus an ethos that continually enacts an attentiveness to, and acceptance of, our limits. Every encounter with an other that is framed by this mode of ontological affirmation is also then a gentle reminder that you will die; and each gentle reminder "helps to fend off existential resentment" at what is often felt to be "the unfairness of mortality." So the cultivation of critical responsiveness is aimed not only at refiguring your relation to the other human but also at "refiguring your own relation to death."[70] Connolly draws again on Nietzsche to explain the latter refiguration. We should, Nietzsche says, learn "To die proudly," "to die freely, consciously, not accidentally, not suddenly overtaken."[71] Connolly seems to want to take these sentiments to mean that if we choose to honor and articulate being as unmanageable presencing, we will also have chosen a kind of noble acceptance of our own death.

Turning back now to Taylor's concerns, can one find anything in the foregoing that constitutes a "draw" toward violence or indifference to suffering? Given other aspects of Nietzsche's aristocratic radicalism, one might be wary here of the image of proudly willing one's own death. Again, such an image could be construed as a sort of distancing gesture, achieved by a purity of will and implying perhaps some disdain for the many who are incapable of this nobility. Whatever one thinks of the possible validity of these suspicions in Nietzsche's case, they just don't seem appropriate in Connolly's.[72] The nobility of such an engagement with

[69] "The Immanent Counter-Enlightenment," 11, 14.

[70] *ID*, 164–66.

[71] Nietzsche in *Twilight of the Idols*, quoted in *ID*, 164.

[72] "The 'overman' now falls apart as a set of distinctive dispositions concentrated in a particular cast or type, and its spiritual qualities migrate to a set of dispositions that may compete for presence in any self. The type now becomes (as it already was to a significant

death is always tinged with a humility arising from an awareness that one cannot really put death on terms of one's own.[73] When Connolly uses Nietzsche's phrase, the power "to die proudly," he follows it immediately with the parenthetical remark "if the unlikely opportunity to do so should present itself." One can't help laughing here, as Connolly no doubt intends.[74] The images of mastering death by aristocratic self-will or by boldly courting it in "limit experiences" are perennial front-runners in the Olympics of human folly. The nobility Connolly would proffer is a modest one, practiced methodically in everyday life, and never too sure of itself.

A propensity for violence would be hard to rivet onto such an ethos. But Taylor might still say that Connolly's honoring of being as unmanageable presencing leaves us a bit too disengaged from some forms of suffering. Although critical responsiveness is highly attentive to how identity/difference dynamics often visit suffering upon constituencies that challenge established identities, it is clear that such cases do not encompass the full range of human suffering. Perhaps Connolly's articulation of his external, amoral source could be said to leave us somewhat indifferent to the suffering of, say, the victims of natural disasters. He might, of course, reply that our reactions will never be entirely free of identity/difference dynamics. But I think he would also have to admit that there are types of suffering where symbolic dynamics do not play an overwhelmingly dominant role, and thus where the obligation of critical responsiveness is relatively idle.[75] In such cases, Taylor might be warranted in pressing his claim about indifference. Compared to his theistic, Christian ethics, with its "divine affirmation" of human worth and its attendant *agapê,* Connolly's affirmation appears limited in the reach of its beneficence.[76]

Connolly would likely have two sorts of things to say here. In self-defense, he might claim that the generosity of his gift-giving virtue could reach to a variety of modes of suffering. But he would also probably freely

---

degree) a voice in the self contending with other voices, including those of *ressentiment*" (*ID,* 187).

[73] Cf. here an important critique by Simon Critchley of any perspective that seeks to make of death a "work"; *Very Little . . . Almost Nothing* (London: Routledge, 1997), chap. 1.

[74] *ID,* 180.

[75] Connolly expresses substantial admiration for the nontranscendental ethical perspective of John Caputo. The latter finds that the direct experience of suffering flesh carries its own immediate call to respond; *Against Ethics: Contributions to a Poetics of Obligation with Constant Reference to Deconstruction* (Bloomington: Indiana University Press, 1993). Although Connolly does criticize Caputo's perspective for being relatively inattentive to the more political modes of suffering highlighted by critical responsiveness, he nevertheless seems aware that Caputo has also pointed out a limit to his own ethics. See *WNS,* chap. 2.

[76] *SS,* 516.

admit that Taylor is pressing him where he is indeed vulnerable. One is always vulnerable somewhere. And the cognitive and affective vivification of this moment of recognition is of utmost importance in a weak ontology. The experience of having your tankful of arguments begin to run dry is one that should be prized, not briskly shuffled aside, for it carries the recognition of why forbearance is a cardinal virtue in the ongoing conversation between those who honor different ontological sources. Each must have recourse at some point to a faith that does not rest squarely on a foundation of sufficient argumentation. In one case it is a faith in God; in the other it is faith "in the ability to cultivate the gift-giving virtue without a god." Recognition of this common condition of interdependence and fragility makes available a new sort of fuel—very slow burning—for adversarial engagements: a respect that reflects a "pathos of distance."[77]

And, if I have read Taylor correctly, he would not find these to be alien sentiments.

5.2.D. Rethinking the Modus Vivendi of Secularism

Although critical responsiveness is perhaps the single most important virtue of the ethos of agnostic democracy, it by no means exhausts the range of prefiguration that Connolly has in mind. Critical responsiveness calls us to attend differently to emerging political identities. But there remains the question of the character of the public relationship between groups and movements whose identity and presence is already established. One of the key elements in Western modernity's answer to this question is its commitment to secularism; that is, to the principle that matters of faith—and thus ungovernable passion—should be consigned to the private sphere. With the emergence of this commitment the discourse of politics was supposed to begin to display a neutrality toward the religions of different groups.

Connolly's case for his ethos of agnostic democracy involves a "cautious reconfiguration" of the principle of secularism.[78] Modern secularism has never, he argues, been quite as modest and neutral as its defenders claimed. To non-Christians and atheists, the secular modus vivendi often had a fairly immodest public agenda. This ambivalent legacy continues to manifest itself today in secularist responses to the pressures of fundamentalization and pluralization that Connolly sees as characteristic of late modernity. The perpetuation of this legacy today creates novel difficulties, however, "when religious, metaphysical, ethnic, gender and

[77] "Rethinking *The Ethos of Pluralization,*" 99–100; *ID,* 85–86, 178–79, 196–97.
[78] *WNS,* 19.

sexual differences both exceed those previously legitimate within European Christendom and challenge the immodest conceptions of ethics, public space and theory secularism carved out of Christendom." Additionally, although "secular liberalism" appears immodest to some constituencies, its responses to contemporary pressures of fundamentalization and pluralization simultaneously seem insufficiently robust to be persuasive in current public debates. With this charge, Connolly seems to be echoing, although nontheistically, Charles Taylor's concerns that secular, neutral liberalism fails to "inflate the lungs of the spirit."[79] In the remainder of this chapter I want first to examine this range of charges, then elaborate the contending ethos of political engagement Connolly wishes to propel into the fray, and finally consider how political liberalism might respond to all this.

The desired barrier between public and private matters, behind which religious passions were to be secured within the modus vivendi of secularism, has traditionally been more porous than many secularists have been willing to admit. Tocqueville's commentary on nineteenth-century North America is somewhat embarrassing in this regard. Even though the United States Constitution seemed to have installed secularism securely at the core of our public life, Tocqueville's reflections suggest that the dampening of strife between Christian sects was achieved "while retaining the civilizational hegemony of Christianity in a larger sense." Explicit sectarianism was kept out of politics, but the ground rules of public reason, morality, and public life were already formed by the generic "mores" (in Tocqueville's words) of Christianity. One only has to think here of how this discursive field constituted the dangerous figure of the atheist. In effect then, even if Christianity was not always explicitly invoked in public life, this was not because the norm of impenetrability was sacred, but rather because, as Connolly puts it, Christianity was "already inscribed in the prediscursive dispositions and cultural instincts of the civilization."[80]

Tocqueville thus supports a secularism that, by its invocation of preconscious mores, remains entangled with ontological sources and the visceral register of being through which they are in part both experienced and articulated. He is accordingly something of an embarrassment to contemporary secularists and something of an encouragement to theological critics of secularism who wish to see public life in the United States once again more firmly centered on an authoritative Christian ethos. Against the background of this dispute, one can begin to perceive the sort of path Connolly's ontology prefigures. He wants, first, to affirm

[79] *WNS,* 19; *ID,* 160–64.

[80] *WNS,* 24.

Tocqueville's appreciation of the force of preconscious mores, without however allowing their "colonization . . . by a civilization of Christian containment." And, second, he wishes to press secularism so that its appreciation of diversity will extend into the realm of sources and registers of being it now gathers under the rubric of "religion."[81]

The predominate strategy of contemporary secularists in the face of fundamentalization and pluralization has been twofold. On the one hand, they have continued to either ignore the visceral register of being or suppress it beneath the level of political discourse. Simultaneously, they have continued to seek ways of updating the "Kantian effect," by which reason can announce its clear, freestanding, unifying authority for public argument, and thereby replace any lingering dependence on ontological commitments, Christian or otherwise. Connolly has in mind here, of course, contemporary philosophers like Rawls and Habermas. The latter hopes to secure the Kantian effect without Kant's appeal to a supersensible realm. The anchor now is that curious "fact" of the "telos of language," from which we can derive a model of rational, practical discourse. For Habermas, we can now be "postmetaphysical," in the sense of leaving ontology behind, and yet still affirm the unshakable authority of this model to adjudicate issues of justice.[82]

A parallel "protectionist" aim is evident in Rawls's effort to ground justice in an overlapping cultural consensus that does not depend on the affirmation of any "comprehensive," and thus controversial, ontological commitments. Rawls thereby offers "a paradigmatic secular tactic for taming conflict: the idea is to dredge out of public life as much density and depth as possible so that muddy 'metaphysical' and 'religious' differences don't flow into the pure water of public reason, procedure and justice."[83]

Secular liberalism today is not only faced with its legacy of unacknowledged, visceral commitment to some Christian fundamentals, but also with a similarly ambiguous legacy regarding the nation. Thus, John Stuart Mill, at the same time he is asserting the significance of individual liberty and diversity, also insists that it is only on the basis of the "common sympathies" of a nation that political democracy is possible. This emphasis on a unifying center of identity, allegiance, and memory as the condition of democracy gives rise, Connolly suggests, to "a liberalism divided against itself," divided because its pursuit of the binding force of national feeling threatens its own commitment to liberty and diversity.[84]

[81] *WNS*, 24–25.

[82] *WNS*, 32, 38.

[83] *WNS*, 22–23. Cf. John Rawls, *Political Liberalism* (New York: Columbia University Press, 1993), xvi ff.

[84] *WNS*, 77, 79–81, 82.

Now Connolly is aware that the existence of some tension between core values is not automatically fatal to a political theory. And yet he wants to suggest that this tension is peculiarly corrosive. When a liberal thinker like J. S. Mill identifies national identity as indispensable to pluralist democracy but cannot "explain how tight, centered or close identity must be to *be* identity," then the image of the nation functions as "a condition to be remembered but never known, pursued, but always absent, absent but never eliminable as an end." We install thereby a sense of political life "in which there is always a black hole at its very center." This "lack at the center provides a standing temptation to some constituency or other to occupy it," proclaiming that "we" embody precisely the characteristics necessary to achieve full national identity. For Connolly, this phenomenon is one of the central visceral dynamics through which fundamentalizing constituencies mark out pluralizing constituencies as threats of the most dangerous sort.[85]

Many contemporary liberals fear this dynamic as much as Connolly. But their responses still cling to the wish to have politics authoritatively centered, even as they seek to immunize it from the more virulent passions associated with nationalism. Thinkers of this sort hope

> to retain the idea of an indispensable center and then respond to the evils of racism, aboriginal displacement, compulsory heterosexuality, and religious conformity *by pulling more and more elements out of the center.* The center now becomes common allegiance to a constitution, a set of rights, the practice of justice, or an authoritative mode of public argument.[86]

Connolly's analysis of the secular liberal response to the will to nationhood has the same aim as his analysis of its response to the resurgence of religious fundamentalism. In neither case does he dismiss the response entirely; rather he wants to highlight some of the costs and risks of these ways of philosophically engaging the forces shaping late modern political life. If he can heighten the perception of such drawbacks, then perhaps the idea of a different general ethos of engagement may sound less presumptuous or utopian.

The drawbacks of secular liberalism arise from its distinctive conjunction of forbearance and desire. Connolly certainly has no problem with ethical forbearance per se; but when it is transformed into "the cardinal virtue of metaphysical denial," it puts liberals at a disadvantage in public discourse, at least when issues such as the legitimate variety of sexual orientation, abortion, capital punishment, and doctor-assisted death are taken up. Political liberals must try to engage such matters while claiming

[85] *WNS,* 81–82, 87; *EP,* 135–37.
[86] *WNS,* 90–91.

they carry no ontological baggage, a claim that appears hypocritical to their opponents. The supposedly neutral, "freestanding" nonontological standpoint is, in fact, a perspective constitutively infused with an ontological desire to hold an authoritative center in the flux of political life. This passion has, however, been rendered so austere that its defenders think it has been released from what they see as the dangerous nexus of desire, motivation, and ontological sources. One is supposedly allowed thereby to have the coherence and unifying bond of allegiance, yet now in a carefully eviscerated mode. But this effort "to cling," in effect, "to the old logic of the nation while shucking off much of its historical filling is to present yourself to many as a weak, uncertain and unreliable defender of the very logic you endorse." If that logic remains in force, Connolly contends, the secular liberal always tacitly invites more virile candidates to push themselves forward as more appropriate embodiments of it.[87]

The desire for a definitive center of public life is what needs to be diffused. However austere it might be, and however thinly that center is imagined, this way of portraying cultural and political life positions contemporary phenomena of pluralization at the periphery of that life. Against this Connolly wants to project a different image of cultural and political engagement, within which there is no authoritative center. For this purpose, he finds Deleuze and Guattari's notion of the "rhizome" quite provocative. They use it in contrast to the "arboreal" notion of a plant with a central trunk from which branches sprout. Rhizomes are plants for which one cannot identify a persisting, deeply rooted center, but rather only multiple nodes with shallow root systems proliferating in multiple directions.[88]

The point of this sort of shift of image is to help cultivate an alternative way of experiencing political communication, contest, and collaboration between constituencies affirming diverse ontological sources. The intention would be to foster a new sort of ethos of engagement that openly acknowledges the visceral dimension of political life and allows the articulation of ontological sources in public discourse. But this articulation hopefully will be joined with a growing acknowledgment of the diversity of sources and thus with a growing willingness to affirm the contestability of any particular source. For those who are moved to such acceptance, the place of the virtue of forbearance changes. It no longer functions as the clear, austere motivational support for walling off ontological sources from political life, but rather as a persistent, uncertain spur to different

[87] *WNS,* 90–91.

[88] *WNS,* 91–93. See Gilles Deleuze and Félix Guattari, *A Thousand Plateaus: Capitalism and Schizophrenia,* trans. B. Massumi (Minneapolis: University of Minnesota Press, 1987), 6–7, 15.

constituencies to embody the appreciation of the contestability of faith and identity "in the *way* they articulate, debate and decide fundamental issues of public life."[89]

In sum, Connolly is asking us to imagine a "new *modus vivendi*" drawn from the prefigurative force of his ontology and the interpretive frame of his account of late modernity. The ethos animating this alternative way of experiencing political engagement, agreement, and disagreement starts not with the orienting idea of an overlapping consensus formed on the thinned-out ground of the unifying idea of the nation, but rather from the rhizomatic experience of cultural density and diversity. One negotiates one's way outward from this decentered experience to a sharing of "overlapping commitments" among constituencies and to certain basic procedures. Now Connolly is under no illusions about the difficulties implied in fostering such a generalized public ethos; nor does he minimize the risks involved. Could patterns of "selective collaboration" arise that are strong enough to support basic rights against fundamentalist attacks? Would theists really exercise forbearance in relation to post-secular Nietzscheans like Connolly? Could patterns of politics in which enmity is turbocharged by existential resentment and "transcendental narcissism" give way to patterns where we cultivate different ways of engaging our political enemies: treating them with "studied indifference" when possible and "agonistic respect" when we have to confront them in struggle?[90]

Clearly, the slow cultivation of such a new political sensibility with its corresponding "political virtues," running from the fullest generosity of "critical responsiveness" to distinctive ways of cultivating forbearance toward competitors, is not going to come easy. Connolly only asks that we set the risks and uncertainties involved over against those of our current configurations of political life.

5.2.E. A Political Liberal Response

How might a liberal respond to the range of criticisms Connolly offers and to the ethos of pluralization he wishes to recommend as a new mode of orientation to self and public engagement? In approaching this question I want to attend primarily to representatives of political liberalism who strongly emphasize its pragmatic, contextualist quality and downplay idealized representations of reasoning or discourse. Both Charles Larmore and Donald Moon tie the validity of liberalism directly to its ability to solve the historically real political problem of clashing perspec-

[89] *WNS*, 38, 95–96; "Rethinking *The Ethos of Pluralization*," 94.
[90] *WNS*, 95–96; 156–61; *AI*, 145.

tives on what constitutes the good for human beings.[91] I focus here on two lines of response to Connolly emerging from this wing of political liberalism. First, I show that it would likely consider some of Connolly's critique simply wide of its mark. In this vein, Larmore could make a reasonably persuasive defense. Nevertheless, I want to suggest finally that with regard to the specific significance of the ethos of critical responsiveness, political liberalism cannot so easily deflect the force of Connolly's claims (section 5.2.E.1). Given this conclusion, I turn to a second liberal response; namely, if the idea of critical responsiveness *is* of real value, then whatever is significant about it can nevertheless be incorporated within political liberalism, without its having to take on any ontological baggage (section 5.2.E.2).

5.2.E.1. Points of Dispute

Larmore and Moon emphasize repeatedly that political liberalism should be understood not only as standing free of any ontological commitments related to a theory of the good, but also as primarily a "strategy" for solving political problems.[92] This strategy involves both moral and nonmoral elements as it seeks to accommodate both the political realm's need for "predictability" and closure, and the modern world's reality of diverging views of the good.[93] Given these constraints, political liberalism asserts that it is reasonable for actors to "bracket" their conflicting views and seek areas of common agreement by a "retreat to *neutral ground*."[94] From that point, actors can proceed by reasoned argumentation toward the general principles of justice of a liberal state that is neutral toward a variety of conflicting views of the good.

When this straightforward strategic quality of political liberalism is highlighted, it casts some doubt on at least part of Connolly's critique. Insofar as that critique depends on the alleged presence in liberalism of an effort to achieve the "Kantian effect," which betrays an unacknowledged ontological desire to occupy an "authoritative center" of moral-political life, it seems to miss its mark. Perhaps that charge will stick to

[91] J. Donald Moon, *Constructing Community: Moral Pluralism and Tragic Conflicts* (Princeton, N.J.: Princeton University Press, 1993); Charles Larmore, *Patterns of Moral Complexity* (Cambridge: Cambridge University Press, 1987), and *The Morals of Modernity* (Cambridge: Cambridge University Press, 1996).

[92] Larmore, *Patterns of Moral Complexity,* 50; Moon, *Constructing Community,* 45–47, 98.

[93] Regarding his vision of the political realm, Larmore says that "system" is "more desirable than sensitivity" (*Patterns of Moral Complexity,* 40). At one point (xv) Larmore speaks of the influence of Niklaus Luhmann on his formulations, by which I assume he means the general systems approach to social theory, according to which the proper function of the subsystem of politics is to reduce the complexity of its environment in order to manage it more efficiently.

[94] Ibid., 53; *The Morals of Modernity,* 125–27; and Moon, *Constructing Community,* 62–73.

Habermas or Rawls, but it is less apt in relation to Moon or Larmore. (In this regard, Moon states unequivocally: "The transcendent aspirations of Rawls's original position or Habermas's ideal speech situation must be abandoned.")[95] If this is so, then it also becomes less easy to believe Connolly's assertion that liberalism's quest for an authoritative center tacitly encourages extreme nationalists to come forward claiming they offer a more satisfying, full-blooded articulation of that desire for a center.

A second aspect of Connolly's critique concerns difficulties arising from the entanglement of political liberalism with the general movement of secularism in the modern West.[96] To a degree both Moon and Larmore would admit this entanglement, at least in the sense that both see Locke's ideas on religious toleration as the crucial initial move in the heritage of political liberalism. The latter seeks to generalize the strategy Locke employed of constituting the political out of the commonality that can be discovered after abstracting from controversial issues.[97] But this general entanglement of secularism and political liberalism does not make the latter necessarily culpable for the specific historical failures of the secular state in the United States. Consider the example of doctor-assisted suicide. It seems to me that Connolly is dead right that the almost total prohibition of such assistance in U.S. law at the beginning of the twenty-first century is a testimony to the power of generalized Christian mores that is operative despite our officially secular status. But political liberals actually seem as adamantly opposed as Connolly is to this failure to recognize such a right. Their opposition is expressed in standard liberal language: the decision about death is certainly a fundamental one; and such decisions are best made by the individual, although the state can legitimately establish safeguards to ensure that a given decision represents an individual's carefully considered conviction.[98] Thus, on this issue and ones like it that Connolly discusses, such as gay and lesbian rights, the political liberal might argue that the difference between them is not as substantial as Connolly implies. It is probably correct to say that on a variety of current, substantive policy positions there would be no sharp

[95] Moon, *Constructing Community,* 100.

[96] Connolly does not, of course, claim that secularism and liberalism are synonymous (*WNS,* 10).

[97] Larmore, *Patterns of Moral Complexity,* xiii; *The Morals of Modernity,* 134; and Moon, *Constructing Community,* 8.

[98] This position was expressed in an amicus curiae brief filed in two cases before the U.S. Supreme Court in 1997, involving the question of assisted suicide. The signatories included prominent procedural and political liberals. See Ronald Dworkin, Thomas Nagel, Robert Nozick, John Rawls, Thomas Scanlon, and Judith Jarvis Thomson, "Assisted Suicide: The Philosophers' Brief, with an Introduction by Ronald Dworkin," *New York Review of Books,* March 27, 1997, 41–47.

divergence. This line of response might not disturb Connolly overly much; he does, after all persistently describe his position as a kind of liberalism, albeit a "reconstituted" one.[99] But, if the foregoing is correct, it means one must turn elsewhere to find the heart of the reconstitution.

So far, I have suggested that some of Connolly's criticisms of political liberals do not strike their target and may in fact show that the two views are closer than he admits. When it comes to the specific idea of critical responsiveness, however, what looks like a core difference between the two comes into focus. The argument, it will be recalled, is that the liberal conception of justice is deaf in crucial ways unless it draws upon the ethical sensibility of critical responsiveness. In short, political liberalism cannot relegate this sensibility to the confines of a particular ontology or conception of the good, over against which liberal justice stands neutral; rather, liberal justice reveals itself as intrinsically limited in a way toward which it cannot, in good conscience, be indifferent.

The initial force of this argument has been admitted by Moon, who recognizes that the sensibility embodied in critical responsiveness is indeed crucial to liberal justice. However, he also contends that this sensibility can be understood as already incorporated into a suitably formulated political liberalism in a fashion that requires no ontological turn.[100] Moon is especially sensitive to Connolly's challenge at this point, because he is deeply aware that strong claims about liberal neutrality, like Larmore's, do not ultimately fit smoothly with the pragmatic, problem-solving view of political liberalism. The neutral, bracketing strategy is certainly affirmed by Moon; but he is also aware that the image of a smooth closure that solves "the given problem," as Larmore puts it, is never a frictionless solution and never comes to pass without the implicit constitution of new problems. He emphasizes therefore what he calls a "tragic" quality to political life. Too bold an affirmation of neutrality induces a deafness to what is left unattended to by any given problem-solving strategy.[101] In effect, Moon is pointing up the irony of professing to operate with a pragmatist notion of validity and then implicitly shoving one kind of *persistent problem* below the level of philosophical consciousness.

Thus Moon is admirably open to taking seriously a range of difficulties that face political liberals. The specific challenge raised by Connolly is, to repeat, that the strategic, rule-oriented conception of justice is flawed unless it draws upon the sensibility of critical responsiveness; it remains

[99] *ID*, 83, 91; *WNS*, 10.

[100] Moon, "Engaging Plurality: Reflections on *The Ethos of Pluralization*," *Philosophy and Social Criticism* 24 no. 1 (1998): 70–71.

[101] Moon, *Constructing Community*, 10, 62–73; and Larmore, *The Morals of Modernity*, 135.

too "stingy" when confronted with new and inchoate challenges to established constellations of perspectives and identities (which constitute the terrain of "given problems"). And the articulation and cultivation of this sensibility draws crucial sustenance, in turn, from the affirmation of an ontology of unmanageable presencing.

5.2.E.2. CAN POLITICAL LIBERALISM INCORPORATE CRITICAL RESPONSIVENESS?

How might political liberalism incorporate the ethos of critical responsiveness and thereby undermine the distinctiveness of Connolly's claim? As I said earlier, liberals imagine the political problem of justice as being engaged by actors who are operating with a minimal moral motivation along with the nonmoral, strategic ones. Moon quotes T. M. Scanlon's interpretation of the moral core involved here: one must aim "to justify one's actions to others on grounds they could not reasonably reject."[102] Fulfilling such an aim, Moon contends, "requires [the kind of] critical responsiveness to specific others" that Connolly espouses. In other words, the commitment to justification implies the duty to display the functional equivalent of critical responsiveness. This is true because you need to find out enough about others in order to decide what they could "reasonably" reject and accept.[103]

I think there is something subtly, but crucially wrong with Moon's claim here. Liberalism overreaches itself when it tries to swallow in one bite the whole of critical responsiveness. Moon has indeed located the place at which liberalism opens out toward an ethos of critical responsiveness, but that is not the same thing as full, effortless incorporation of its insights. Where he goes wrong is in failing to see a significant difference between the character of the motivation animating the foundational commitment of political liberalism and the character of the one animating a critical responsiveness embedded in a weak ontology.

The example through which Scanlon introduces his motivation of morality is instructive in this regard. He asks us to consider our reaction to a famine in a less developed part of the world. We affluent Westerners can typically be brought to feel profoundly the weight of a failure to aid the victims, especially when doing so would have such a low cost to ourselves. This sense of being "crushed" testifies to our discomfort at

[102] Moon, "Engaging Plurality," 70. Scanlon's argument is made in "Contractualism and Utilitarianism," in *Utilitarianism and Beyond*, ed. Amartya Sen and Bernard Williams (Cambridge: Cambridge University Press, 1982), 116. In this article, Scanlon refers to this moral core in terms of a "desire" we have. In his more recent work, he speaks of an "aim"; see Scanlon, *What We Owe Each Other* (Cambridge: Harvard University Press, 1998), 6–8, 32–33. I don't think this change affects the force of my argument.

[103] Moon, "Engaging Plurality," 70; cf. Larmore, *The Morals of Modernity*, 136.

finding our actions not to be in accord with our belief that we ought "to be able to justify our actions to others on grounds they could not reasonably reject." Now this particular way of representing the weight of the motivation of morality offers an interesting insight as to its peculiar character.[104] It seems that morality involves an aim that is constitutively entwined with something like anxiety before the bar of justification or a sense of guilt at having not acted rightly. I desire to *protect myself* or *free myself* from moral discomfort and guilt (actual or potential) by means of the activity of justification. I desire to demonstrate that I have adhered to the rule of reasonableness; but it is an anxious desire. My point here is not to criticize anything substantively about Scanlon's analysis of this crucial dimension of moral experience; it is rather only to become clearer about the specific character of the liberal motivation of morality.

Returning to Moon's argument, the key question now becomes the following: Would this sort of motivation be likely to animate the array of aesthetic-affective and ethical techniques and endeavors that Connolly's perspective encompasses? I have my doubts. Let me hang those doubts around a couple of features of the political liberal's motivation. First, as I just noted, such motivation unfolds with a concern for self-protection that tunes one's aesthetic-affective responses in ways that don't align easily with the sensibility of critical responsiveness. The rule of justifying *my* actions carries an aesthetic-affective dynamic appropriate to a world where identity matters have been solidified into fixed centers, making discrete claims upon one another. This hardly seems to be conducive to the risky, exploratory, decentering techniques of the self Connolly is envisioning.

There is, second, something ill-fitting in *how* the political liberal's motivation *moves* one. The requisite aim of justifying oneself supplies, as it were, a relatively rough push toward engagement with the other. Specific conduct—such as giving arguments—is mandated as a means to the end of justificatory release from possible counterclaims that the norms upon which I act are not reasonable. Contrast this with the way one is moved through the ethos of critical responsiveness. One is less "pushed" by the imperative of rule conformance to adopt its techniques and practices than one is "drawn" to take them up as ways of articulating the ontological source of generous, unmanageable presencing. Such conduct is not simply a means to an end, but is also valuable in itself. Every act taken and disposition cultivated is expressing some adhesion (stickiness) in relation to that source, in the sense—as Taylor so nicely puts it—of both discovering and creating its meaning.

[104] Scanlon, "Contractualism and Utilitarianism," 116.

But perhaps political liberalism would be less susceptible to the foregoing line of criticism if one were to interpret its moral core somewhat differently. Larmore, for example, appeals not so much to the imperative of justification, as to the simple idea of "equal respect."[105] Adherence to a norm of equal respect might easily be imagined as both incorporating the obligation to display something like critical responsiveness to others, and as doing so in a way that might not have the same motivational dynamics as the Moon-Scanlon reading of liberalism's moral core. In short, for Larmore, we are simply responding to human dignity, something that does not seem to involve so deeply the gravitational field of self-protection and anxiety about being left without justification in the face of the rule of reason. I would suggest, however, that the same sort of difficulty does in fact arise, and thus that one cannot simply extrude the sensibility of critical responsiveness out of the bare notion of equal respect any more plausibly than out of the idea of an imperative of justification.

Consider the aesthetic-affective dynamics that adhere to this unique sense of respect. Crucial here is Larmore's remark that his norm of equal respect "comes close to the Kantian rule" that we should treat people as ends rather than means.[106] The two norms are not exactly identical, because Larmore is not following Kant in positing a noumenal world of pure rational beings, before which one stands in transcendental awe, but rather attending to the natural qualities of reason and freedom. Nevertheless, there is something about these particular natural qualities that continues, as in Kant, to give the notion of humans as ends in themselves its capacity to move us in a peculiarly compelling way. What sustains the attractiveness of the idea of equal respect is the notion of encountering the other human as something unique under the sun. This uniqueness constitutes our sense of human dignity, and our recognition of that dignity occurs with a distinctive force. Kant understood this force as a sublime feeling of elevation.[107] I think that someone like Larmore who separates out equal respect as the core of morality is implicitly trading on this sublime force as part of the affective circuitry that runs through his efforts to legitimate his position. It is not the sublimity of the noumenal in a strict sense, but rather the sublimity of the other as that wonder of nature: a rational, self-reflective creature.

When Kant invokes the sublime in this regard, he of course wants to quarantine it from all sorts of other morally relevant feelings; otherwise

[105] Larmore, *The Morals of Modernity,* 136.

[106] Ibid.

[107] Kant, *Grounding for the Metaphysics of Morals,* trans. J. W. Ellington (Indianapolis: Hackett, 1993), 22 n. 2, 33, 43, 46. The corresponding pages in the standard German edition

it could lead to a contamination of the self-governing moral agent by entangling her with all the unruliness of human affect.[108] Whatever persuasiveness one accords to this isolation strategy in Kant, it would seem to have no purchase at all in an appeal to equal respect that posits no noumenal world. Consequently, one must think the force of the sublime here as not neatly containable within the bounds of Kant's narrow philosophical role. According to a tradition running back to Edmund Burke, the force of the sublime has usually been understood to involve not just sheer elevation, but also a related feeling of fear and anxiety, pain of some sort.[109] When one includes these aspects of the sublime, one begins to see the aesthetic-affective dynamic of equal respect in an additional light. There is not just the edifying feeling of elevation, but also the force of being called to account, being hauled before the judgment of other rational creatures. Involved now are feelings of wariness, self-protection, and uneasiness at discharging ones obligation to justify oneself at this bar of judgement. Kant's word for "respect"—what stands at the center of his morality—is "Achtung." In everyday German usage, this word typically carries connotations of: wake up, be aware, be on guard, get yourself in order.[110]

At this point, I would suggest that we are on the same moral-aesthetic terrain as earlier. In other words, the effort to unpack the moral motivation of political liberalism in terms of equal respect does not move us from where Moon was operating. We are still being pushed to account for ourselves, haunted a bit by guilt and anxious about protecting ourselves. Again, as I emphasized above, my point is not to denigrate the elevating force of a figuration of the other (and myself) as creatures of reason and freedom. Rather it is to probe more carefully the full character of this field of force that is brought to bear when one centers morality on notions like the duty of justification and equal respect. And when one attends to this full dynamic, one will see that it is simply not conducive, *by itself,* to an effective cultivation of a sensibility like critical responsiveness.

are *Grundlegung zur Metaphysik der Sitten* (Berlin: Preussische Akademie der Wissenschaften, 1900–), 4:411, 425, 439, 442.

108 Kant, 46 (German edition, 442).

109 See Edmund Burke, "A Philosophical Inquiry into the Origins of Our Ideas of the Sublime and the Beautiful," in *The Works of the Right Honorable Edmund Burke* (Boston: Little Brown, 1881), 1:106–11. I am aware that Kant did not think much of Burke's "merely empirical exposition of the sublime." But I would suggest Kant did not help us by forcing this topic to conform to his notions about the noumenal. See Kant, *Critique of Judgment* trans. with an introduction by W. Pluhar (Indianaopolis: Hackett Publishing , 1987), 138.

110 Cf. Scanlon, *What We Owe Each Other,* 269–72, where he relates guilt in morality to the fear of failing to be adequately self-governing.

To sum up, Moon is correct in recognizing the intrinsic limits on political liberalism's efforts to find completely neutral ground; and he is correct to emphasize the significance of attending to the voices that are unavoidably backgrounded in the necessary search for reasonably neutral ground; but he is not correct to think that political liberalism can effortlessly incorporate that mode of attentiveness Connolly calls critical responsiveness. This would appear to indicate an exposed flank of liberalism, a place at which it cannot quite get itself free of the need for the input of richer ontological figuration.

One now has a better way to understand Connolly's appeal to a "dissonant interdependence" of critical responsiveness and more familiar conceptions of justice.[111] Thus, starting from political liberalism's conception of justice, I have shown that it opens out toward the ethos Connolly affirms but cannot smoothly incorporate it. But if one now reverses the starting point of reflection, how exactly does the ethos of pluralization open itself out toward justice? Here Moon offers an interesting criticism that seems to raise some question as to the adequacy of critical responsiveness. If that ethos is to open toward justice, one has to be able to point to something in it that would "lead to the motivation of morality," in the sense of drawing us toward a willingness to "constrain what we may do by the need to justify our actions to others."[112] I think Moon has a point here. Among the micropractices and dispositions of critical responsiveness, there is nothing that draws us clearly in the direction of such motivation. But this insight is not as fatal as Moon thinks. That is because his critique here is actually very close to the one I developed earlier (section 5.2.C), which suggested that Connolly needs a better ontological figuration of the sense of doing justice to others. That figuration, which I sketched around the way that an utterance calls us, creates a plausible prefiguration of a duty to justify ourselves to others. Were Connolly to accept the additional ontological figure, it would supply the needed sense that critical responsiveness opens out toward justice. But the richness of such a figure has implications beyond this particular role of prefiguring the constraint of rational justification; that is, it does more work than Moon has in mind. This is because the utterance is not figured here merely as the embodiment of some discrete claim on the part of a being conceived as a self-governing, self-protecting entity. The utterance is rather always also entangled as well with the world-disclosive appearance of meaning. And this disclosure is never free of inarticulacy; it remains

[111] *EP,* 186–87.

[112] Moon, "Engaging Plurality," 70.

always a moment in an ongoing process of ontological articulation. When one understands these further features of my figuration in the context of Connolly's notion of the unmanageable presencing of being, one can see the way in which that figuration nourishes not only the imperative of justification but also the tentative, risky, decentering, and exploratory micropractices of critical responsiveness.[113]

[113] When the focus is on the utterance as world-disclosive as well as expressive of self-governance, the sense of sublimity that is involved is expanded further. Now the force of the sublime is not only a constellation of feelings of elevation, fear, and anxiety but also of feelings of mystery, unexpectedness, and inarticulacy emerging from the insight that the other, and myself, are never fully articulate, self-contained, or self-governed. It is to the force of this aspect of the sublime that I would look to aid in cultivating critical responsiveness.

CONCLUSION

I HAVE BEEN TRYING to show two things. The first is that there is a weak ontological turn going on today in political theory. My strategy was to put together in a lineup some unusual suspects who share the characteristics of weak ontology. If my reconstructions have been successful, then the field of contemporary theory should look a little different.

I am also aiming to show that there is something particularly persuasive about contributions to moral and political theory that understand themselves in these terms; that is, I have been elucidating the strengths of weak ontology vis-à-vis its competitors. In conclusion, I want to say a bit more along these lines. Weak ontology primarily challenges three other modes of thinking that inform contemporary political reflection: strong ontology, postmodernism or poststructuralism, and political liberalism.

Strong ontologists are likely to categorize the claims of weak ontology as a new variant of nihilistic, postmodern attack on ultimate values. But if my interpretation of Taylor is correct, it should make this sort of swift rhetorical riposte a good bit less sure of itself. Taylor's value in this regard lies in his powerful elaboration of a theistically rooted moral and political theory that is articulated nevertheless in weak ontological terms.

In relation to postmodernism or poststructuralism, the core issue I have raised is how one challenges various fundaments of modernity without that critique becoming an imperative disconnected from affirmative moral and political formulations. I have argued that to be persuasive in a sustained sense, such formulations must draw explicitly upon ontological sources. Many poststructuralists and postmoderns seem undecided between jettisoning ontology wholesale and appealing obliquely to one that is somehow different. Simultaneously, they tend to want to relocate the affirmative moment of political thinking into the idea of a politics "to come." Within this model, political reflection shuttles between excoriating critique of an irredeemable present and "messianic" appeals to an indefinite, but somehow redemptive, future.[1] As a result, the careful, risky, and plodding work of affirmation migrates toward a receding horizon. One upshot of my reading of Butler is to show that, by articulating

[1] Derrida emphasizes this notion of the "messianic" in *Spectres of Marx: The State of the Debt, the Work of Mourning, and the New International,* trans. P. Kamuf (New York: Routledge, 1994); see also "Of an Apocalyptic Tone Recently Adopted in Philosophy," *Oxford Literary Review* 6, no. 2 (1984).

and augmenting her ontology, she has developed more resources for such work, thereby drawing off some of the normative overload otherwise carried by her own appeals to the "futural."

Political liberalism is usually not seen as having much in common with poststructuralism or postmodernism, but they do agree in being skeptical about sustained ontological reflection. Political liberalism does not condemn ontology as bankrupt; rather it holds ontology at arm's length. It declares itself neutral toward all ontologies, whether they affirm God or the disengaged self. From the standpoint of weak ontology, this claim of neutrality is not taken to be totally misguided, but rather just more limited than its proponents imagine. When the heart of political liberalism is taken to be a straightforward, pragmatic proposition (as I did in the last chapter), then this philosophy represents a powerful position on the late modern terrain of political thinking. But I hope to have shown in the chapters on Taylor and Connolly that it must be more modest in its self-understanding than it sometimes is.

Taylor helps one to see more room for legitimate constitutional variation than political liberalism would normally allow. In the present context, it is crucial that his argument does not simply affirm a view of the good and derive some political principles directly therefrom. Rather, he interprets Western modernity as an ontological space of conversation and affirms—in weak-ontological fashion—one corner of that space. In so doing, he stakes out a position that cannot be peremptorily disqualified by political liberals.

Connolly helps one see another limit of political liberalism. In chapter 1, I claimed that one of the characteristics of weak ontology is its attentiveness to the aesthetic-affective dimension of human being. But I realize now, after completing my reconstructions, that this characterization is not sufficiently specific. Weak ontologists affirm a specific type of sensibility. I pursued this topic most persistently in the discussion of Connolly and liberalism. Connolly's critical responsiveness is a sensibility that cannot simply be subsumed under the liberal values of equal respect and tolerance. We do better to understand the latter as very specific virtues, not as infinitely elastic ones. Although I developed this point only in relation to Connolly, I realize now that it applies as well to the other thinkers I considered. Each presses, in his or her own way, the significance to late modern democratic life of an ethos or sensibility that is more generous in its attentiveness to others than tolerance and respect alone. We see it in Butler's appeal to "a more open, even more ethical kind of being," in Kateb's "democratic aestheticism," and in Taylor's understanding of generosity in the conversation of humankind.

Thus the involvement of weak ontologies with the aesthetic-affective dimension is of a particular character. Substantively, we are called to variants of an ethos that would have us engage the strangeness of the late modern world more receptively. Political liberals are likely to ask at this point—as well they should—what difference this kind of ethos will make to the basic constitutional structure of the liberal democratic state. When such an ethos is bundled with appeals to a "futural" legitimacy, as in Butler's case, we may think we are being urged toward a radically new politics. But my sense is that this ethos does not cast wholesale doubt upon constitutional structures. Rather it points us primarily toward different ways of living those structures (as Taylor puts it), perhaps living them in a less "stingy" way (as Connolly puts it). All this remains, no doubt, somewhat vague. The hope I share with these weak ontologists is that if more people were to cultivate this sort of receptive ethos, then the feel and outcome of at least some types of everyday political interactions would be significantly affected.

INDEX